Dedication

In loving memory of my mother and father
and
My sisters and brothers, nieces and nephews, for their
incredible support, unconditional love, and encouragement.

Rediscover the magnanimous spirit within—
and the power you already possess to
miraculously transform your life.

Contents

Imperishable Truth!

A perfect moment in time where it all makes perfect sense!

A simple shift in consciousness
An indescribable beauty
Difficult to imagine
Impossible to define
Beyond the limitations of our imagination

The world
A cleverly crafted game
Full of color and hidden treasures
A marvelous creation
And our temporary home of residency

The body
An amazing instrument
Meticulously constructed
A highly engineered transport vehicle
And the sacred temple to our true aspirations

The mind
An ingenious design
Capabilities abound
An intricate tool
And our inner mirror to where true riches are stored

Our spirit
The core of our earthly pursuit
Eternal and divine
A vast well
Where unconditional love, happiness, and peace prevail

Flying high
Looking down

Watching people struggle
Trying so hard to be!

Why can't people see?

Flying high
Falling from grace
Far from everything
Conscious of everything

Two worlds separated by unnecessary illusions
Two worlds intertwined as one!

Torn in the middle
A self-destructive existence
A world in dire straits!

Beautiful souls lost in the depths of darkness
Beautiful souls waiting to be free!

A bright light shines along the horizon
But no one seems to know which way to go!

Afraid of the unknown
Afraid to let go!

The Golden Age is coming
We've got the keys to the kingdom
The key resides deep within our true desires

Cast all fears and doubts aside
Take a leap of faith

What have you got to lose?

A bright light is about to shine in the world
A new world is about to unfold!

A beautiful existence full of surprises
A precious gift waiting to be unraveled

A marvelous creation
It's a shame to deny!

Imagine everyone truly working together—All as one
Where unconditional love and peace prevail
No judgment, selfishness, or greed

The possibilities are infinite
Anything is possible!

The human mind
Our ultimate battle!

Surrender all doubts and fears
Walk forward fearlessly

Trust, Surrender, and Believe

A bright light shines along the horizon
It's drawing nearer to help us see!

An indescribable beauty
Difficult to imagine
Impossible to define

A beautiful feeling that grows and subsides all time
No beginning and no end!

A beautiful world
Full of wonder and marvel

An undeniable truth
A recognition that we yearn for and desire!

Miracles will occur and astound
Light will shine in the darkest places!

A miraculous world waiting to be revealed
Hidden treasures waiting to be discovered

Cast all fears and doubts aside
Walk forward fearlessly

The escape route leads to nowhere!

Life
Boundless beauty
Infinite possibilities
A precious gift
And a grand opportunity to rediscover ourselves anew!

The sun will shine again in all its brilliance!

Everybody wants to be
It's not until we realize
We already are
Everything that we are striving to become

The power is within
To just simply be!

Anything is possible
We can be whatever we want to be

Stay in the moment
Enjoy the moment

Trust and Believe

Surrender all doubts and fears
And truly be free
To just simply be!

Chapter 1

Our Divine Life Purpose

To rediscover ourselves anew and truly be free.

Life is full of choices, opportunities, and infinite possibilities. As human beings living a physical existence, we have incredible power and potential. We are highly sophisticated and intelligent examples of life-form living on our planet; and as a result, are capable of effecting the most profound change—not only in our personal life, but in the world around us. What we can perceive, we can usually achieve with the correct use of creative energy and willpower. The problem is, however, that too often we fail to see the wondrous beauty in life and allow our limited beliefs and attitudes, sociological conditioning, and external circumstances to interfere and dominate our true desires, affecting our state of being in the world and the choices we make. This choice of submission denies us our power and privilege to consciously create and live the life of our dreams.

Unfortunately, in our modern world, we too often depend on our external reality and fallible physical senses to determine how we interpret and interact with the world around us. Generally, without our conscious awareness, we allow unsubstantial and contradictive authorities to easily influence our mind and determine how we conduct ourselves. This dependence can create a conflict with our true desires, and unnecessary blockages on our journey to true enlightenment.

The problem is, we live in an embellished world that too often teaches us to look outside ourselves for happiness and fulfillment—causing us to deny our true nature, creative power, and potential. The main focus and motivation for life is then based on materialistic attainment and personal advancement, creating a conflict with our spirit and stifling our spiritual progress. If we want to lead a more rewarding and fulfilling existence, it's important that we start to become consciously aware of the core of our innate nature and infinite source of power, allowing it to become an unequivocal guiding force in our life.

In order to reconnect with our innate nature and experience the true beauty of our most natural and supreme state of being, first and foremost we need to realize and appreciate that we exist beyond the physical level of existence. As human beings, we're made up of three parts: a mind, a body, and energy. I will often refer to this energy as our *spirit* or *soul*. The important thing is to recognize that the core or essence of our innermost being consists predominantly of energy or light, and it is here that our true power and wisdom resides. Primarily, we're energetic or light beings temporarily occupying a physical body.

Unfortunately, in our modern world, we are apt to dismiss or underestimate the energetic part of our being and the impact of energy in our daily lives. Too often, we tend to view the world through a very narrow lens or a limited perspective. Basically, we allow our external reality, made up mostly of matter, to influence and determine how we view ourselves and the world around us without opposition. This limited perspective can restrict the natural flow of energy, limiting the infinite possibilities and opportunities available to us. If we want to lead a more rewarding and fulfilling life, it's important that we start to recognize and value the impact of energy in our everyday existence.

Energy, or divine light, is the vital life force that sustains our being and permeates our existence. Everything in the universe exists as a form of energy or consciousness. The consciousness of a human being is but a small fragment of a greater universal consciousness or higher intelligence that interconnects all life on our planet and beyond. Energy vibrates at different frequencies and becomes denser, vibrating at a lower frequency as it transforms into matter. Physical matter can only exist due to the exertion of energy, and energy must exist before matter can form. We require energy to influence and shape matter. Physically, every movement we make and every word we speak requires a certain amount of energy to be sustained and fulfilled. Our thoughts are also forms of energy that are transmitted into the universe and help to shape and create our reality. We can influence and mold energy through the power of our thoughts. Fundamentally, energy is the driving life force behind our existence. Without this invisible force, our world would fail to exist. It is energy that allows us to come into form and create our desired reality.

The biggest problem in our modern world is that we neglect this simple truth, and as a result, have a tendency to consider ourselves purely physical beings, or tend to focus predominantly on the physical part of our being. This limiting idea or perspective can create all sorts of conflicts and struggles, as it does not reflect our true nature and potential. It denies us our innate power, and the potential to create the life of our dreams.

To help highlight and understand the effect of this limiting idea, we need to examine our energy, or spirit, exclusively, without the weight of our mind and body.

First, we need to understand that our spirit or energy is the conscious part of our being that exists independent of physical form and beyond the limitations of the mind and body. It is the part of us that is all-knowing and connected to the greater universal consciousness or higher intelligence of the universe. It has a divine intelligence and subsists beyond the physical level of existence. Our spirit is superior to matter, as it is our energy that influences and creates matter.

The possibilities of our spirit to change our life are immense. It has the power to transform thought into matter instantly. It is the logical mind or intellect, which usually interferes and creates unnecessary doubt, fear, and confusion in our life. Our spirit can see beyond our physical and self-imposed limitations and is always guiding us toward our highest truth and divine life purpose.

If this energy or energetically conscious part of ourselves simply existed, without mind and body, we wouldn't really know our infinite source of power and potential. To truly know ourselves and understand the power we already possess, we need to experience it through form or matter. It is only through experience that we can understand and rediscover our true identity and unlimited potential.

In order to get to know ourselves and our true identity, we're given a precious gift—*life on Earth*. This provides us with a grand opportunity to use our power to influence and shape our physical world. The Earth plane is like a cleverly crafted game that we agree to play to help us rediscover our true essence or identity.

When we enter the Earth plane, or physical level of existence, we're stripped of any conscious awareness of our true selves or our true identity. This provides us with a unique and grand opportunity to experience ourselves anew. We forget that we are ultimately spirit, and that our main objective in life is to rediscover and live this simple truth. It is through our situations and experiences that we progress spiritually or energetically, learning to live a spiritually empowered and awakened life.

The Earth plane consists of solid matter; therefore, in order to physically interact with our environment, our spirit is encased in our body. The physical body has no conscious intelligence of its own. The body simply acts like an obedient servant and a highly engineered transport vehicle. It is the sacred temple where our true aspirations reside. The body is responsible for carrying out the spirit's desires. The healthier the body, the better the spirit can reveal and express itself.

We also have a mind that enables us to interact emotionally and intellectually within our physical environment. It is through our emotions and experiences that our spirit grows and rediscovers its true nature and potential. Here, it's worth pointing out that the mind doesn't have the wisdom and superior intelligence or knowledge of the spirit. The power of the spirit is inconceivable, and beyond the limitations of the reasoning mind or intellect.

Unfortunately, in our modern world, too many of us succumb to the authority of the logical mind and allow it to take control, creating a conflict with our true desires and stifling our spiritual progress. The spirit becomes trapped in the confines of the human mind and finds it difficult to surface and truly illuminate our life.

In order to live a more spiritually empowered and awakened life, it's important that we understand how the human mind works, and how too often our limited thought patterns, inherited or adopted beliefs, and attitudes can very often overshadow our true desires and interfere in the creation process. This creates unnecessary blockages on our path to true enlightenment, happiness, and fulfillment.

The mind
Our main control center
Where the initial seed of manifestation is planted

The mind
Our ultimate battle

To regain divine control and conscious awareness

To reprogram our database
To remove obsolete and outdated programming
To refresh our outlook

To allow our true desires to freely surface
To walk forward fearlessly
And actively create our desired reality

To fulfill our divine life purpose
And live in perfect bliss, peace, and harmony!

Chapter 2

The Power of the Mind

*We are like unsuspecting directors creating our own reality—
the greatest script of all.*

The mind is a highly sophisticated and complex organ
beyond human intellectual comprehension. It's responsible
for processing everything—including retrieving memories,
storing information, acquiring knowledge and skills,
interpreting our senses, formulating thoughts and patterns of
behavior, initiating body movements, and controlling our
breathing. The brain is the core element of all conscious and
unconscious process, an essential component that defines our
humanity, and an important part of our being. The mind is an
amazingly powerful tool at our disposal, and our most
important ally in the creation process. In the physical world,
the mind acts as our personal power center and controls our
level of awareness and consciousness.

Everything in the universe exists as a form of
consciousness. The consciousness of a human being is but a
small fragment of a greater universal consciousness or higher

7

intelligence that interconnects all life on our planet and beyond. Human consciousness exists independent of physical form. Before anything can exist in physical form, it must first exist as an idea or thought in awareness or consciousness. Through acceptance, initiation, and the correct use of creative energy, it can then begin to take on a physical form.

Our most dominant thoughts, beliefs, and attitudes will very often control our level of awareness and consciousness, which helps shape our reality and determines the parameters that co-exist within our physical world. Generally, what we focus on and believe to be true is usually what we will attract and create in the world around us. It is, therefore, important that we understand how the mind works and how too often our restrictive thought patterns, acquired beliefs, and attitudes can very often overpower our true desires and interfere in the creation process, creating unnecessary blockages and preventing us from taking the necessary steps to transform our dreams into reality.

The human brain is separated into two hemispheres or thinking parts: a left brain and a right brain. The different parts of the brain deal with different functions and aspects of our life. The left side of the brain is analytical and orderly, processing information in a linear and sequential manner. It depends heavily on logical sequence and detail, predominantly relying on the interpretation of our five physical senses of sight, sound, smell, taste, and touch.

The left side of the brain is usually directed outward, depending exclusively on its connection to our physical world and reality. It is limited in its perspective and cannot see or conceive beyond our environmental limitations and constrictive identification to our physical existence. Basically, it cannot transcend its own limitations of spatial and temporal relations. It is bound by our individual identification and attachment to our physical world. As a result, our divine inner being and inexhaustible well of infinite creative energy or power is altogether unknown to the intellect, or the left side of the brain.

Fundamentally, the left side of the brain operates like a computer that we program. When we're born, the left side of the brain is like an empty hard drive on a brand new computer, with infinite potential and storage space, available for individual programming and customization—although, like a computer, it is usually only as good as the person using it.

Our physical world and external reality will help program and shape our logical mind, or the left side of the brain. The media, our upbringing, life experiences, traditions, and other often embellished authorities will help influence our mind and affect how we view ourselves and the world around us. The left side of the brain will store all of our personal experiences, acquired knowledge, and adopted beliefs into "files." It will usually react and respond to life situations accordingly, often without our conscious awareness or inference.

In contrast, the right side of the brain is creative and artistic. It operates through the same creative power as the higher intelligence and absolute consciousness of the universe. It is capable of processing and interpreting multisensory input or information simultaneously, predominantly relying on our all-inclusive sixth sense or extrasensory perception. It uses feelings, holistic thinking, imagination, and intuition. The right side of the brain personifies our true nature and yearns to express and reveal itself. It is the side of the brain the spirit uses to communicate our true desires.

We often experience the right side of the brain when we transcend our physical level of existence and slip into an altered or heightened state of consciousness or awareness. This shift in consciousness can be consciously induced and experienced through various techniques or disciplines such as meditation, and can also happen spontaneously throughout the day while we're engaged in our everyday activities.

When we experience this altered or heightened state of consciousness, we're no longer constricted or bound by our physical existence and our attachment to the physical world. We become free to experience the archetypal mind.

The choice of which side of the brain is in control during different situations defines our personalities and determines our character. It also strongly influences how we react and respond to life. Unfortunately, in our modern world, the left side of the brain often tends to dominate, and dismisses or invalidates anything of significance coming into consciousness from the right side of the brain—just like a computer cannot respond to an unknown command or prompt.

When we rely exclusively on the left side of the brain, we lower our vibration to the purely physical level of existence. Basically, we allow our external reality, habitual thoughts, acquired attitudes, and beliefs to strongly influence the choices we make and how we conduct ourselves. All the little things we repeat to ourselves on a daily basis have the greatest impact on the life we experience and the reality we create.

All of our most dominant and habitual thoughts and beliefs become deeply ingrained in our subconscious mind and act like a filter system through which we view the world and ourselves. All of our experiences in life are usually filtered through these thoughts and beliefs. They will strongly influence and determine how we do things, what we say and don't say, how we react and respond in different situations, what we accept and what we reject, the opportunities we see and fail to see, and the decisions we make.

Most of us are unaware of this process, as it occurs on a much deeper level in the subconscious mind, without our conscious awareness. The problem is that most of our thoughts and beliefs are outdated and limited by nature. They don't always reflect our true potential, or account for spirit working behind the scenes in truly mysterious and miraculous ways to create our highest good. As a result, too often we refrain from following our heart's true desires. We continue to think and act in the same old, outdated way—achieving the same old, outdated results.

Generally, what happens is that our spirit will impress our conscious mind with a perfect idea, thought, or image. If we do not simply trust, and act on, our intuition (the right side of the brain), we allow our rational mind (the left side of the brain) to intervene and try to work out how things will happen. Unfortunately, it will not have all the information, making it difficult to process, and as a result, will often be very quick to dismiss or abort the idea as too good to be true or impossible to achieve.

The left side of the brain likes to know how things will occur. Generally, everything needs to fit into a neat little package. Unfortunately, most inspired ideas don't always come in a neat little package with a step-by-step guide up front, whereby each step of the process is known in advance and the outcome is assured. They usually only provide the next step in the process and require us to trust and have faith in the unknown.

The left side of the brain, relying heavily on logical order and sequence, finds these ideas difficult to digest and, if we allow it, has a tendency to go into overdrive, thinking about every possible scenario. At this point, if we don't learn to monitor our thoughts and take control of our mind, it can go into a frenzy, overwhelming us with conflicting ideas and at times preventing us from confidently following our intuition.

Unfortunately, in our modern world, too many of us don't consciously realize and respect the power of the mind, and we underestimate the impact of our thoughts on our reality and the choices we make. Some of our acquired thoughts and beliefs are so deeply ingrained—particularly those that we've carried since early childhood or those that adhere to mass global consciousness—that we simply accept them as truth. Our logical mind doesn't have the wisdom or superior intelligence to realize that they don't reflect our true nature and potential. In fact, most of our problems and struggles in life can be attributed to limiting thoughts and false beliefs that we hold about ourselves and the world.

If we want to change what we create in life, we need to learn to become more consciously aware of the thoughts and beliefs we support, as well as the functioning of our mind. Once we do so, we can begin to develop a more harmonious relationship with the left and right hemispheres of the brain, allowing us to take greater control of the thoughts we allow to dwell in our mind. We will no longer need to allow our opposing thoughts to influence the choices we make and determine how we live our life, creating disharmony with our spirit and stifling our spiritual growth. We can start to attract new circumstances and situations that nurture our spirit and reflect our true potential. Our current external reality is the result of past thoughts, beliefs, and actions. We have the power to change our external world by simply changing our internal world of thoughts, attitudes, and beliefs.

Our external world is a reflection of our internal world. We cannot expect our external reality to change if we don't change our internal reality of our thoughts and beliefs. If we want to change our external reality, we need to change our internal reality. Only by changing our internal reality of thoughts and beliefs can we expect our external reality to change. If we continue to think and act in the same old, outdated way, we will continue to achieve the same old, outdated results over and over again. When we change our thinking patterns, we naturally change the way we feel and do things, which naturally leads to a change in a result or outcome.

It's like a computer that's no longer performing at its optimum or achieving the desired results. When this occurs in real life, we don't simply keep using the same computer or programs, as this would affect the outcome. Instead, as technology advances, we also tend to upgrade our computer or software. It's usually in our best interests to achieve the best possible result. In the same way, we need to challenge our existing thoughts and beliefs to reflect our personal growth and the evolution of our planet.

Purifying our mind and reshaping the way we think is of paramount importance to changing our life and the world we inhabit. By clearing and purifying our mind, we can begin to free ourselves from erroneous thoughts and beliefs that too often hold us back, preventing us from achieving our goals and realizing our potential.

Through freeing our mind and developing more positive ways of thinking, we can begin to liberate our infinite source of creative energy and power, and positively change our world. It's important to remember that even though our thoughts and beliefs may strongly influence and create our reality, we have the power and ability to choose *which* thoughts and beliefs we allow to reside in our mind.

Every moment in life is a choice. How we make that choice will strongly influence how we experience the world around us.

As human beings, we have free will. The free-will choice gives us the opportunity, in every moment, to choose which thoughts and beliefs we will entertain and support.

Our spirit will very often communicate our true desires and intentions to us, usually through our intuition, but it will not impose or interfere with our choice. To interfere would be to take away our free will. Our spirit will even attract particular situations, people, and things to help us realize our dreams, but we must consciously decide the path we walk, taking the necessary action to bring our dreams to fruition. It is only through our emotions, choices, and free will that we can continue to spiritually evolve and experience the truth of our innate nature and potential.

Ultimately, it is up to *us* whether we continue to fall victim to the countless thoughts running through our mind, or take back control and make the necessary changes in our way of thinking—thereby creating and living the life we desire and deserve.

Understanding the creative power of the human mind and how it works is crucial to taking greater control of our life. When we learn to tap into the creative power of the mind, we will find that it is an amazingly powerful instrument, and our most important ally in the creation process. If we disregard the power of our mind and do not learn to control our thoughts, the mind can become our worst enemy—creating unnecessary confusion, obstacles, and hardship on our path to true enlightenment, happiness, and fulfillment.

The other day, I planted a seed
At first, there were no signs of growth

Each day I watered my plant and gave it love

Several days later it started to sprout
And each day I watched it grow a little more

One day it started to wither
But I did not panic
Instead I stayed focused and
continued to water my plant and give it love

I never gave up hope
Even when it looked like it was about to wither away

Now,
the
Seed
has
fully
grown
and
Each
day
I
Enjoy
the
Fruit
From
the
tree.

Chapter 3

The Creation Process

*Our thoughts are like little seeds of manifestation, and the
harvest we reap depends mostly upon the seeds that we sow or
the thoughts that we allow to dwell in our mind.*

We are creative beings by nature, and the creative energy
of our thoughts and feelings invariably helps to shape our
reality. The most frequent thoughts that we allow to pass
through our mind usually have the greatest impact upon our
life and the world we experience. The more attention we give
our thoughts, the more we energize them, allowing them to
take on a physical form or emotional state. Our thoughts are
like magnets—we are either entertaining positive thoughts
and thereby transmitting positive energy, or thinking negative
thoughts and thereby emitting negative energy into the
universe. What we attract back into our lives is often
reflective of the thoughts and beliefs we mostly support and
entertain.

The universe doesn't distinguish between positive and
negative thoughts. It simply registers our thoughts and

responds by reflecting back to us what we're thinking by drawing people and circumstances to us in accordance with our most habitual thoughts and beliefs. The universe always responds to our every desire. What we think and believe, we will usually attract and create. Creating reality is a fundamental faculty of the mind. It is where the initial seed of manifestation is planted. Thus, by changing our thinking patterns and beliefs, we can change our reality and state of being.

Our thoughts are forms of energy that strongly influence the world we create and experience. All energy vibrates at a particular frequency, and each thought has a different level of vibration. What determines the frequency of our thoughts depends upon our beliefs and attitudes, and what we're thinking at the time.

Our thoughts also have magnetic powers and operate in much the same way that magnets do. When we transmit our thoughts into the universe, the universe absorbs this energy and responds by attracting or magnetizing to us all things that are on the same frequency, or that are in accordance with our most dominant or habitual thoughts.

When we focus on positive thoughts, we radiate positivity, emitting a frequency that attracts people, things, circumstances, and situations that complement our positive beliefs and attitudes. Conversely, when we focus or dwell on negative or imperfect thoughts, we begin to vibrate at a lower or slower frequency—attracting people, things, circumstances, and situations that resonate with our negative attitudes, thereby reaffirming our negative thought patterns. This gives them strength, allowing them to interfere in the creation process.

In order to change our reality, it's important that we begin to take greater control of our mind and become more consciously aware of the thoughts we allow to dwell in our mind. Our feelings can very often provide valuable insights into our innermost thoughts and beliefs, which enable us to carefully monitor and control our thinking patterns.

Our thoughts strongly influence how we feel and how we conduct ourselves. When we think negative or imperfect thoughts, we cut ourselves off from our divine source of energy and power. As a result, we generally experience a lack of life-force energy flowing through us. This can often leave us feeling deflated, unmotivated, and even depressed. These negative states naturally lower our personal vibration, making us even more susceptible to negative and draining influences. This can often create a downward spiral, making it difficult for us to regain control and raise our level of awareness to higher planes of thought.

In contrast, when we think independent and positive thoughts, we bring ourselves into closer alignment with our divine source of inner power and creative energy, allowing life-force energy to freely flow through us—energizing our mind, body, and soul. As a result, we generally feel motivated, energized, and alert. This surplus of energy allows us to operate from a position of inner strength and power. Our thoughts not only affect our personal state of being, but also have a profound impact on the rest of the world.

Every thought engages with the energy of the universe and helps to shape and influence the world around us. The most frequent thoughts we choose to collectively entertain ultimately influence our physical world. Essentially, negative or destructive thoughts seek out and bind with other negative thoughts on the same frequency. When we concentrate on negative things, we give them power and strength, allowing them to take on a physical form and co-exist in our world. Essentially, the more power and energy we give something, the greater the issue usually becomes.

On the other hand, positive thoughts seek out and combine with other positive thoughts on the same frequency. This naturally creates an excess of positive energy, helping to eliminate the effects of negative and destructive energy. If we all collectively thought perfect and harmonious thoughts, we would live in a perfect and harmonious world. Unfortunately, this is not usually the case in our modern times.

Too often we focus our attention and energy on those things we don't like or things we lack, therefore giving them strength and allowing them to interfere in the creation of our desired reality. We tend to focus our attention on the obstacles we may encounter, rather than on the joy and fulfillment we experience from transforming our dreams into reality.

If we want to attract love, abundance, and happiness, we need to start to *focus* on love, abundance, and happiness. Only when we do so will we proceed to create a life full of joy.

When we begin to understand the creative power of our mind and the impact of our thoughts on our reality and state of being, we can begin to take greater control of our life and the world we create.

We simply need to make an active and conscious decision to become more aware of our thoughts and habitual thinking patterns. We need to shift our thinking and focus from negativity and lack, to positivity and abundance. We all have the innate ability and power to choose positive thoughts—and the natural birth right to enjoy abundance.

Basically, we need to regain divine control of our mind and become more proactive participants in the creation process. This doesn't need to be a difficult task. We simply need to be open to new and improved ways of thinking and being. By choosing more positive and expansive thoughts and beliefs, we can begin to transform our life and the world for the better. Thoughts are a relatively light form of energy and, therefore, can easily be changed.

We can eliminate negative thoughts and beliefs by simply replacing them with more positive thoughts and higher truths that serve and nurture us rather than enslave and drain us. By recognizing negativity and replacing it with positivity, we take away its power, preventing it from manifesting in our lives and affecting the way we operate in the world. The most important factor in creating a more rewarding and fulfilling future is to *always* remain positive.

Positive thinking simply involves having a mind full of loving thoughts, where imperfect thoughts struggle to survive or exist. Love is the greatest power in the universe and the highest frequency we can emit. Love energy connects us with our soul and the creative energy of the universe, and all good things in life and the world are created from love energy. Our power to create thoughts of love is unlimited. Love energy creates and sustains life. It inspires and empowers us to live as an authentic reflection of our authentic selves, freely expressing and following our true desires without fear of judgment, ridicule, or failure.

As we begin to think more positive thoughts and higher truths, we will naturally start to vibrate at a higher frequency. As we begin to vibrate at this frequency, any negative thoughts we hold about ourselves and the world will naturally start to dissolve and fade away. This is because negative energies cannot sustain themselves in the realm of higher and faster vibrations.

In a perfect world, positive thinking would come naturally and easily. Unfortunately, life isn't always like that. Sometimes good things happen and sometimes not. Sometimes situations might occur that make it difficult for us to remain positive, but these are the times when we *most* need to practice positive thinking. The key is to always remain positive no matter what situation we may be facing. Remember, positivity is a state of mind. It is not something that *happens* to us or is dependent on things or situations outside of our control. It is simply a choice of perspective. Negativity—regardless of the situation we may find ourselves in—never serves us. It only tends to make things worse. It's important for us to practice positive thinking until it becomes a natural way of being. As you will read about in the next chapter, the repetitive use of positive affirmations is an effective way to retrain our mind and create resourceful and empowering states of being.

I am worthy and deserving.

I live life as an authentic expression of my true self.

I radiate true inner beauty.

I am eternal and divine.

I believe in myself.

Anything is possible.

I can be anything I want in life, and I have the strength and power to overcome all obstacles.

I am given everything I need to accomplish my goals.

I am always connected to the divine power and unconditional love of my spirit.

Life is beautiful and full of wonder.

Every moment is a grand opportunity to allow my spirit to shine in all its magnificence.

Life is a precious gift, and I appreciate every moment.

I am a resourceful and creative being made up of love and light.

I always keep an open heart and mind.

I respect and care for all living things.

I trust and believe in the natural rhythm and laws of the universe.

Chapter 4

Positive Affirmations

Every thought we think, word we speak, and movement we make is an act of creation that strongly influences the world we create and experience.

An affirmation is any positive statement that we make or declare to ourselves as being true. Positive affirmations give us the power to reprogram our thinking patterns, allowing us to change the way we think and feel about ourselves and our world. When we say or think positive affirmations, we create positive statements that we can refer to on a daily basis. The repetitive use of positive affirmations is a powerful and effective way to retrain our mind, creating resourceful and empowering states of being. Affirmations empower us to identify and move through emotional blockages and restrictive thought patterns that too often prevent us from fully embracing our power and living the life of our dreams. In short, positive affirmations can help us transform our life and nourish our mind, body, and spirit in many uplifting ways.

Positive affirmations work by reprogramming our mind and by changing our thinking patterns. The practice of engaging in positive affirmations allows us to recognize and replace some of our negative and worn-out self-talk with more positive thoughts, attitudes, and beliefs that reflect our true nature and potential. When we make an affirmation, we replace our thoughts and beliefs with new, higher truths and beliefs. The aim is to recognize and transform negative or restrictive thoughts, attitudes, and beliefs into positive and expansive ones that naturally reflect our authentic selves. Saying positive affirmations directly affects our conscious and subconscious mind, and we can reprogram our mind through their proper use.

The best way to reprogram our mind is to learn to become more consciously aware of our thinking patterns throughout the day. In this way we can learn to catch our negative and restrictive thoughts as they arise, and replace these thoughts and beliefs with higher truths that reflect our spirit and ultimate potential. For affirmations to have the optimal effect, it's important that we state them in the most positive and effective way possible. Affirmations work like commands given to a computer. When we state our affirmation, the subconscious mind and universe register our intentions as stated and act accordingly. Thus, the way we construct our statement is of paramount importance to the outcome.

When making affirmations, it's best to use positive words in phrasing them so they can make the most immediate impact. Affirmations are most effective when stated in the present tense, as we always want to say them as if what we're affirming has already happened, even if this is not actually the case. That is, we don't want to say, "I will have a wonderful relationship," which keeps the dream in the future, but rather, "I *have* a wonderful relationship," which places the concept in the present. Also, negative words are less effective than positive ones. For example, instead of saying, "I never have money problems," it's best to say, "I enjoy financial abundance."

Similarly, let's imagine for a moment that we're dissatisfied with our current job situation. In order to attract a more rewarding and fulfilling position, it's important that we declare our affirmation in the present tense. If we state, for example, "A more rewarding and challenging job will come to me," it keeps this prospect in the future. The universe will register our thought as stated and will not respond immediately. Since we want to attract this opportunity *now*, in the present, we need to state our affirmation or intention in the present tense. For example, "A more rewarding and challenging job comes to me now." This allows the universe to act immediately on our behalf, perhaps creating a more fulfilling position in our current workplace, or alternatively drawing to us a more exciting and rewarding new job opportunity.

Each word contains its own energy, and the way we phrase our affirmations will strongly influence the outcome. Basically, positive words create positive energy and empowering states of being in the world. Negative words create negative energy and disempowering states of being. If, for example, we want to improve a health condition, we shouldn't focus on the illness itself and state, "I am recovering from _____ [insert condition]. The mind will register and probably focus on the word describing the condition, giving it strength and power. Basically, we're reinforcing the problem, not the solution.

To attract and create perfect health, we need to *focus* on perfect health. As an example, the best way to overcome a health condition is to focus on perfect health and start to see ourselves as healthy. We should think and state positive affirmations such as: "I radiate perfect health," "I am strong and healthy," "I am perfect in mind, body, and soul." The use of positive words and thoughts will help reinforce our intention and create the best possible outcome. As we begin to focus on perfect health, we will naturally start to feel healthier.

It's important, at all times, that we remain focused on our

intention and do not give energy or power to any lesser or underlying thoughts or beliefs that may begin to surface, interfere, or create blockages in the process.

While stating or thinking affirmations, it's important that we continue to carefully monitor our thoughts and feelings. This will enable us to review and update our affirmations to reflect our progress, and eliminate any underlying thoughts or beliefs that may arise while we learn to adopt new and improved ways of thinking and being.

For example, if we affirm, "A more rewarding and challenging job comes to me now," but do not truly believe that this is possible, or that we're not worthy enough, these deeply ingrained thoughts could interfere in the manifestation process, closing the doors to more promising and rewarding opportunities. It's important that we acknowledge these deeper thoughts and beliefs and keep reaffirming any necessary affirmations until they're removed from our mind. For example, it's best to state: "A more rewarding and exciting job comes to me now," "I am worthy and deserving of a good opportunity," and " A new position comes to me easily and effortlessly." We must fully believe that our affirmations are true and possible for us before they can have any real impact on our lives. The more we feel and see ourselves as the way we *want* to be, without any doubt or fear, the sooner we will start to attract positive change into our daily lives.

When we first start to use affirmations, we may experience some form of skepticism or apprehension. These are usually automatic responses that may arise from our resistance to change, or our fear of the unknown. We may also find ourselves quickly slipping or reverting into old patterns of behavior and ways of thinking. This is because many of our thoughts and beliefs have become deeply ingrained in our subconscious mind after years and years of repetition.

The key is not to become discouraged if this happens or if we don't see tangible results immediately. Most of us have years and years of negative thoughts patterns that may need to be acknowledged and healed, so it may take time to change some of these lifelong habits. We need to be gentle and patient with ourselves. Stating and thinking positive affirmations is a process that requires *patience*, *practice*, and *perseverance*. The subconscious mind is very receptive and will eventually adapt itself to our new and improved ways of thinking.

The subconscious mind has no power of induction. It simply accepts whatever the conscious mind sends it. Hence, if we make a conscious decision to change our thinking patterns, habits, and beliefs, the subconscious mind will simply accept it. The best way to impress the subconscious mind with our new and improved way of thinking is achieved in the same way we created the old ones: through repetition. Repetition is the key to affirmation success.

The repetitive use of positive affirmations will help rid us of old restrictive thought patterns and push through even the strongest resistance. The continual repetition of an affirmation, stated with conviction and passion, will eventually ensure its adaptation by our subconscious mind. Remember, repetition and practice makes perfect.

There are many ways in which positive affirmations can be used powerfully and effectively. We can say them to ourselves or out loud throughout the day or night. We can practice saying positive affirmations while walking, waiting for a bus, driving a car, cycling, or sitting on a train. We can even dedicate specific quality time to saying positive affirmations each day—perhaps before we go to sleep or when we wake up in the morning. Making positive affirmations in the morning is a particularly positive and empowering way to start the day.

We can also say our affirmations out loud or to ourselves while looking at ourselves in the mirror. This technique is especially useful when dealing with personal issues that we may need to address or heal—particularly with regard to self-love, self-esteem, self-confidence, or self-acceptance.

At first, we may feel uncomfortable, as issues may arise

that we've managed to comfortably suppress or successfully avoid—particularly if we're not used to facing ourselves in the mirror. As these issues or emotions start to surface, we may begin to feel uneasy or out of balance, and as a result, be tempted to turn away.

However, it's important that we persevere and stick with the affirmations, allowing our issues to come to the surface and be healed. If we don't release these suppressed emotions, they will continue to impact us in our everyday lives. Only after we acknowledge and release these repressed emotions will they cease to have any more power over us. And, we will naturally start to feel freer and lighter and allow our true nature to shine forth.

We can also write down or type our affirmations. When writing them down, it's a good idea to really focus our attention and think about our words to help impress the subconscious mind. Once we've written down our affirmations, we can read them out loud or silently repeat them to ourselves throughout the day and night. We can also post them in our bedroom, bathroom, kitchen, car, or other places where we spend a lot of time. This acts as a powerful visual trigger, serves to reinforce our intention, and helps to truly impress the subconscious mind.

The trick is to be creative and experimental when making positive affirmations so we can discover which way works best. We are all different and learn in different ways. What works for one individual may not necessarily be best for another. The key is to be adventurous, using whatever means possible to maintain a positive and healthy state of mind.

Thinking and stating affirmations is an effective way to consciously practice positive thinking and retrain our mind. Through controlling the functioning of our mind, we can begin to exercise greater control over our lives. Positive thinking is something we should learn to cultivate and strive to achieve every day, in every moment. By practicing positive thinking habitually, we create an enlightened state of mind, which creates and attracts positive things into our life. We should continue to consciously practice positive thinking until it becomes a natural and automatic way of being.

In essence, if we have a mind full of positive thoughts, we will create a life full of positive things. As you will see in the next chapter, creative visualization is also a powerful and effective technique that can help strengthen and support our affirmation practice.

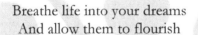

Breathe life into your dreams
And allow them to flourish

Believe in your dreams
And take the necessary steps to make them happen

Follow your dreams
To where true happiness awaits!

Chapter 5

Creative Visualization

*Trust, surrender, and believe in the infinite creative
power of the universe that made the vision possible—
anything is possible.*

Creative visualization is a powerful mental technique using
the power of our imagination to bring about positive changes
in our life. The process of creative visualization allows us to
consciously harness the unlimited power of our mind and use
it in a positive way to effect real change in our own lives and
the world at large. It simply involves creating a mental image
or idea of something and focusing on it. By doing so, we give
it power and strength and make it real, which helps us attract
what we desire.

We all have the ability to visualize, and the depths of our
imagination are endless. The only limitations are the
boundaries we impose upon ourselves. Creative visualization
gives us the opportunity and power to consciously choose
which ideas, images, and thoughts we allow to occupy our
mind. The mind is like a huge Doodle board. If we don't like

the image in our mind, we have the power to simply wipe it clear and create a new picture with the help of our imagination. The mind is where the initial seed of manifestation is planted, and the first step to transforming our ideas and dreams into reality.

We tend to attract whatever we think about or visualize most strongly. Thoughts, ideas, and images are all living energies that are transmitted into the universe and strongly influence what we create. Before anything can appear in the physical form, it must first appear as an idea, image, or thought in consciousness or awareness—and this always precedes manifestation. For example, "I need a holiday" is the idea or thought that usually comes before the necessary arrangements. Thus, simply by having a thought, idea, or image and holding on to it in our mind will very often lead us to take the necessary steps to transforming it into reality.

The reason why creative visualization is so powerful is because as we focus on the picture or idea, giving it positive energy, we begin to create equally powerful thoughts and feelings. This brings the image to life in the present moment as though we already have it, sending out a very powerful signal to the universe. The universe will naturally respond by drawing to us all those things, people, situations, and circumstances that are in alignment with what we're visualizing as true in our life at the time. The stronger our visualization, the more powerful it is, and the more likely it is to become a reality.

The same principles used with positive affirmations can be applied to creative visualization. The most important step in both processes is our *intention*.

As human beings, we have free will and the creative power to bring about whatever we desire. In fact, what we intend to happen—whether it be on a subconscious or conscious level—is usually what we attract and experience. Therefore, it's important that we think about what we desire and hope to achieve *before* we begin the process. A clear and compelling intention is of primary importance if we wish to have a positive outcome.

Intention is one of the greatest creative forces in the universe. It has an enormous impact on the reality we experience. When we have a strong and clear intention to create something, it is usually very likely to manifest in our life in one way or another. The clearer and stronger our intention, the more likely we are to achieve our goals and experience success. It's equally as important to take into account that we usually manifest what we desire more readily when our intention is pure, and in alignment with our highest life purpose and the will of our soul.

Creative visualization always works best when our ideas are born of divine inspiration, aim to improve the quality of life for all, and are not simply fueled by selfish desires. We should never wish harm on another or do anything that may impact others in a negative way. For example, if someone is causing us distress or conflict, whether it be at work or in a relationship, we should always ask that the situation be dealt with and resolved in a loving way, for the highest good of all concerned. Remember that what we try to create for someone else will usually always boomerang back to us sooner or later. It's also important that we *believe* in what we intend in order to achieve and maintain a positive attitude throughout the process.

Once we set our intention, we need to surrender and have total trust in the universe to act on our behalf. We shouldn't consume valuable energy worrying about the details. It isn't our responsibility to work out *how* things will happen. If we do so, we remove ourselves from the present moment and disconnect ourselves from our divine source of creative energy, power, and inspiration.

Our analytical mind, which cannot transcend its own limitation of spatial and temporal relations, more often than not finds it difficult to work out how things will occur. As a result, it can very often go into overdrive, thinking of every imaginable scenario, and things that may never actually happen. This can create unnecessary conflict, anxiety, and worry—preventing us from taking the necessary steps to realize our dreams. Similarly, we should not expect things to happen in a preconceived manner or anticipate the outcome. By doing so, we limit the many wonderful ways in which the spirit works to bring us exactly what we need.

The creation process simply requires us to trust, surrender, and believe that the universe will act on our behalf and always provide for our highest good. The universe has a superior knowledge and divine intelligence, and is capable of conspiring in truly miraculous and ingenious ways to make the right things happen, at the right time.

When we simply choose to surrender, trust, and believe in the power of the spirit, we allow its creative energy to freely filter into our conscious mind. This provides us with the inspiration and guidance to transform our dreams into reality.

We also need to keep an open mind and be willing to change or re-evaluate our goals, should life start to naturally take us in a different direction. The universe always provides for our highest good and responds to our every desire. Sometimes, however, things don't always go as we expect, or there's a time delay. This can often stir doubt and confusion within us, testing our faith and patience. During these times, we must remain true to ourselves and focus on our intention, allowing our inner vision and strength to guide our way.

At times we have limited information on hand, and what we consider to be the best thing in the short term may not necessarily be the best outcome in the long term. For example, let's imagine that in the process of seeking a new position, we submit an application to a high-profile company within our current area of expertise, but become very dejected when we aren't called for an interview. Several months later, a more attractive opportunity becomes available that suits our needs and requirements perfectly, allowing us to develop and explore our creative potential in a new and exciting way.

If our initial application had been successful, we may have

missed this better opportunity, which was just around the corner. We might have gotten stuck in a position that wasn't in our best interests in the long term, and probably would have caused subsequent discontent.

So often what initially appears to be a disappointment actually turns out to be a blessing in disguise. The universe truly works in miraculous and mysterious ways. The key is for us to remain open, and be willing to follow our intuitive nudges, no matter where they may lead. We need to remain positive at all times and allow ourselves to be open to receiving. We shouldn't become discouraged if we don't see tangible results immediately. We must learn to give our dreams the time they need to blossom and flourish. Time is a valuable teacher, and patience is one of the vital lessons we need to learn in order to live a spiritually empowered and awakened life.

Worthwhile dreams take time to build and cannot be rushed. Being patient helps us develop the ability to live fully in the present moment. Life isn't about living in the past or anticipating the future. It's about fully accepting and living in the current moment, and doing what we can with what we have. Patience is, therefore, an integral part of living a truly fulfilling life.

To have patience is to have faith in the natural flow of life, and to work in harmony with the natural rhythm and laws of the universe. When we do so, we're almost always assured success. We usually only encounter pain and suffering when we try to transgress the natural laws of the universe. Sooner or later, good things come to those who wait and who do the right thing. Of course, this doesn't mean that we should just sit around and wait for things to happen. We still need to work hard to achieve our goals, but we also need to appreciate that sometimes it may take time before we experience a positive outcome.

Creative visualization is a useful technique that allows us to remain focused on our goal. It's a practical means to success, as it grants us direct control over our mind, allowing us to harness the power of our imagination and use it in a resourceful and positive way. This allows us to effect genuine, lasting change in our life.

Living in the moment
Freedom and liberation
No separation
No expectations
No demands
No greed
No worries

Living in the moment
Unaffected by trials and tribulations

Taking one day at a time
Enjoying every step of the way

A beautiful and continuous journey
Of being present in each and every moment!

Chapter 6

Living in the Present

Life is a continuous journey of being present in each and every moment.

The present moment in time is where we are in the here and now. It is the centerpiece of balance between the past and future. The present is the only moment in time that can be perceived or experienced directly and fully by engaging all of our senses on a mind, body, and soul level. It is the only moment in time in which we can fully interact with our environment and the world. It's impossible for us to be in any other place except where we are in this very moment in time, in the here and now. We cannot physically be present in the past or future. We can only think about these states in our mind. Thus, the past and future are only mental concepts that we formulate intellectually. They have no real power in the present moment unless we choose to think about them, which gives them attention and power.

To successfully center ourselves in the present, we must fully engage ourselves in the moment, without letting our mind wander off into the past or race ahead into the future. Unfortunately, given the demands of modern living, this is not usually the case for most of us. Instead, our mind tends to be preoccupied with thoughts and worries about the past and/or future.

These days, we have a tendency to dwell on the past, or project our thoughts into the future. In fact, most of us tend to spend most of our time just about anywhere else other than the present moment. Very rarely do we truly let go and experience the wonderful joy, freedom, and liberation that the current moment has to offer. Rather, many of us allow our mind to wander, and we're constantly thinking about something other than what we're actually doing. As a result, we're often too influenced by the countless thoughts running through our mind to truly appreciate the true beauty that surrounds us in the here and now.

It can be difficult to still our mind and focus our attention for long periods of time without the mind wandering off, or being easily distracted by the allure of the modern world. In fact, if the mind is left to its own devices, it will tend to wander off aimlessly and start to think about all sorts of inconsequential things. This can consume valuable energy and steal our attention away from the present moment.

When we do not live fully in the now, we disconnect from our inner source of power, guidance, and wisdom. Basically, we allow our mind to become preoccupied with our physical existence and be overburdened by the demands of the minutiae around us. This is not productive, does nothing to serve our divine life purpose, and can have an undesired effect on our overall state of being.

It's important that we learn to control the functioning of our mind and thoughts and bring back our focus and attention to the present moment when we find ourselves unnecessarily drifting off into the past or future. We shouldn't allow ourselves to become consumed by thoughts and worries that have no relevance in the immediate moment. A wandering mind is often an unhappy mind. When we think about the past and future, we miss the beauty of living in the present, as well as the opportunity to experience ourselves fully and completely.

The past has already occurred; we can't change what has already happened. We can only learn and grow from it. It's only a memory that exists in our mind, and it has no real power in the present unless we choose to think about it. When we remove ourselves from the present moment, and give our past problems attention, we energize them, giving them power and strength. This can very often have an undesired and overwhelming effect on our emotional and physical well-being.

Our physical body has no conscious intelligence of its own and simply responds to what is going on in our mind. The mind, depending on what we choose to think about and believe to be true, can stimulate and trigger powerful feelings and emotions that can ultimately affect our emotional, mental, and physical health.

This altered state of being can obstruct our ability to think and see clearly. It can also strongly influence how we respond to what is going on in and around us—affecting the situations, circumstances, and opportunities we create for ourselves in the present. We don't need to get stuck in the past, allowing past misfortunes and outdated patterns of behavior rule how we behave in the present. The true beauty of living fully in the moment means that we liberate ourselves from the past and become free to be who we want to be in the here and now.

For example, if we had a tendency to be shy in the past, we need not allow this behavior to affect the choices we make and the opportunities we create today. Living in the present allows us to disassociate ourselves from restrictive thought patterns, attitudes, and behaviors that too often debilitate us, preventing us from fully embracing the now. Every moment in life is a grand opportunity to experience ourselves anew and live fully in the present moment—free of worries and concerns about the past and future.

There's also no point in constantly projecting our thoughts into the future. This creates anxiety about things that have yet to be created and experienced. Rather, it's best to be practical about what may arise and set goals that we work toward in a positive way, rather than constantly fearing what may come up tomorrow, next month, next year, and so on.

The future can only be imagined. What we desire today may be very different tomorrow. Our circumstances may also change—that is, what may not seem possible today may be possible tomorrow. Tomorrow may also reveal something new or different, changing what we hope to achieve today. We never know what tomorrow may bring, so we might as well keep an open mind and remain in the present. Our future very often depends on what we do in the now, as our current thoughts and actions will strongly help to shape and determine our tomorrows.

Our present circumstances are the result of *past* thoughts and actions, and the future will be the result of our *current* thoughts and actions. Therefore, we must remain positive, mindful, and aware in the moment. We should always keep an open mind and not get stuck in the past or future, missing the opportunities that present themselves today. Basically, we should not allow the illusion of time to take hold of us and hinder our spiritual progress, which can unduly affect the choices we make.

When we remove the concept of time from our mind, we're able to live in the present moment, which simply means that our awareness is completely centered in the here and now. It means being aware of what we're doing, how we're feeling, and what we're thinking. If we're not living in the present, we're living in illusion. The only place we can effect real change in our lives is in the present moment. Thus, it's important that we start to recognize and nurture the power we already possess, and learn to use our creative power wisely to live the life we truly desire and deserve.

The power of living fully in the present moment is huge, because when we do so, the continual motion picture running through our mind, and the incessant chatter of our thoughts, begins to slow down. With practice and discipline, we can stop these thoughts from occurring altogether, allowing us to reconnect with our true nature. This quality of release, free from attachment to the past and concerns about the future, brings with it the greatest sense of liberation. This is empowering, as we naturally begin to experience a heightened state of consciousness that is accompanied by a profound sense of inner peace and tranquility.

In this elevated state of consciousness, our sensitivity is also heightened; and as a result, our responses and reactions begin to arise more naturally—and always for the highest good of all concerned. The spirit is already perfect, continuously creating for our highest purpose in life and guiding us toward our essential truth. When we trust in the power and wisdom of the spirit, we can more easily learn to live fully in the present and achieve a state of acceptance and peace. By doing so, we live in harmony with the natural rhythms and laws of the universe, and positive things start to occur effortlessly. The right people, situations, and circumstances are brought to us in their divine right order and time. So, there's no need to dwell on the past or worry about the future.

Every moment in life is a unique opportunity to start afresh and truly live in the light of higher truth. The presence of light and love eliminates darkness and fear. It helps us to see clearly and dissolves all that may still be obscured in our life. It allows us to see for ourselves all the thoughts, feelings, and behaviors we may have harbored in the past that have prevented us from moving forward in a positive way. It also helps provide us with the courage and strength to take the necessary steps to realize our dreams and live life as an authentic expression of our true selves. It enables us to operate in the world from a place of strength and power, giving us the confidence to follow our inner bliss without being affected by past events or worries about the future. Life naturally begins to take on a new meaning and starts to flow with greater ease, synchronicity, and abundance.

Living in the present means living in the here and now, the only moment in time where we can effect real change in our lives and fulfill our innate potential. This is a state of being truly worth experiencing—bringing us greater peace, freedom, and joy. Equally, it is a goal we should all strive to attain in this lifetime, in every day and in every moment.

Find the courage and inner strength
To push beyond fear and self-imposed limitations
And realize your ultimate reality!

Chapter 7

Fears

"Knowledge dispels fear, for fear is born of ignorance. Where there is love and trust and knowledge, there fear cannot reign."
— Silver Birch

Fear is usually an unpleasant feeling—a primal reaction to imminent danger or a perceived risk of danger. It is one of the basic human emotions, and major causes of energy blockages. It can have a huge impact on our mental, physical, emotional, and spiritual well-being. Fear can be inherited from a parent or significant other, particularly during childhood; and when not addressed, can lead to phobias and irrational behavior in adulthood. Additionally, it can be planted through an external source—diminishing hope, confidence, self-worth, and self-belief—preventing us from seeking happiness and expressing our own truth.

Such is the case when we give fear power by engaging with its process. There are two types of fear: real or direct, and irrational or indirect. As long as the danger is direct and real, fear is a normal and healthy physical reaction to help protect us by enhancing a focused and alert state of mind. On the other hand, irrational fear is often an unhealthy response, as the danger is not real or direct and consumes valuable life-force energy to sustain itself. This creates unnecessary blockages on our journey to enlightenment, happiness, and fulfillment. It's important that we learn to distinguish between our rational and irrational fears so that we don't allow the latter to hinder our spiritual progress, keeping us from creating the life that we truly desire and deserve.

Irrational fears are simply illusions of the mind that we impose on ourselves. They serve no direct benefit in our life, as they often stem from erroneous fundamental beliefs and our own uncontrolled, incessant thoughts. Our fears most commonly arise from our fear of failure and our uncertainty about the future. Other common causes of fear include our attachment to the known—that which is comfortable and safe; our constrictive physical existence and material possessions; and our bonds to loved ones.

Typical fears may include simply being afraid of something that cannot actually harm us, worrying about things that we can do nothing to avoid, fretting over situations that we may never actually experience, or trying to exercise control over things that are yet to come into form. Fear is the opposite of trust; and can make us weak, vulnerable, and more susceptible to negativity. We need to learn to monitor our thoughts and eliminate irrational fears that block our inner source of creative energy and power.

The mind likes to chatter, and can often become overpowering in its attempts to try to keep us safe. When we get a new idea, sense, or feeling born from divine inspiration, if we do not simply trust our intuition and act accordingly without fear, we allow our irrational mind to interfere in the process. This can create unnecessary confusion, fear, and doubts. At this point, if we don't learn to control our mind, it can often go into overdrive and start to conceive every conceivable scenario, but that's all it is—an imagined scenario or possible outcome. The problem is that the rational mind relies heavily on logic and detail; therefore, it cannot account for the spontaneity of our spirit to work within its parameters. Should we choose to entertain our negative thoughts and fears, we allow them to take hold of us, which gives them real strength and power. This is not conducive to our divine life purpose, as it can imprison our true desires, creating an overwhelming and often detrimental effect on our well-being.

Our thoughts release chemicals into the bloodstream that match our emotional state. Fear can stimulate and release powerful emotions that are often real and intense, and which can overwhelm and affect our entire being. Fear can prevent us from regaining control over our emotions, as well as our ability to put things into their proper perspective. It's important that we express our emotions, but avoid becoming dependent or consumed by them. We need to learn to separate our higher self from our feelings, and recognize them as energies within their own right. Emotions are real and an essential component of our being. They help us understand ourselves and relate better to others. They also serve to motivate us and provide valuable information with respect to what we're experiencing, guiding us toward change and spiritual evolvement. Thus, we must learn to recognize and express our emotions in a healthy and beneficial way.

Problems can arise when we try to deny or suppress our emotions. They will remain hidden and often create a sensation of heaviness, leading to problems such as sorrow, disappointment, and worse still, dis-ease. For example, if we don't acknowledge and release our emotion of fear, it may prevent us from walking forward confidently, taking the necessary steps to achieve our goals and fulfill our potential. Consequently, we're left with a feeling of dissatisfaction and a lack of fulfillment, simply because we're not doing what we're truly meant to do. Alternatively, when we acknowledge and accept the emotion of fear, we can make a conscious decision to let it go and know that it's only an illusion of the mind. Since it's not real, it has no true power over our spirit. We must learn to accept our emotions as energies within their own right, and encourage them to grow spiritually.

Life is a precious gift that we chose to experience in order to evolve spiritually. It is through our emotions and experiences that we learn and grow. If we were already aware of the outcome of our choices, it would defeat the purpose of our physical existence. Life would become mundane and highly predictable. It would fail to provide us with the same exciting challenges and opportunities for self-realization and spiritual growth. We cannot always control whether things will go our way or not, but we *can* learn to control how we react and deal with given situations. In life, it's important to remember that we will not be given anything we don't already have the power and strength to overcome. It is, therefore, a shame to allow fear to hinder our spiritual progress and prevent us from achieving our goals. We owe it to ourselves to rise above this emotion and prevent it from getting in the way of our happiness.

Fear gives negative energies in our external world a place to attach themselves. Like attracts like; therefore, we're more likely to attract and experience negative situations, people, and circumstances if we're already in a place of fearfulness. It's important for us to clear ourselves regularly of negative emotions and energy that may have an ill effect on us. We should not limit ourselves and allow our fear of failure to get in the way of our success. Our spirit has the power and intelligence to recognize and dispel fear. We need to learn to trust in the power of the spirit to constantly inspire and guide us through all our trials and tribulations.

Our most important task in this regard is to transform our fears into love. When we come from a place of love, we bring in an energy that helps heal and release our fears. Life is too short to allow fear to prevent us from truly living in the way we desire. We deserve to go forward and live our dreams, which will naturally serve and nurture our higher being and ultimate purpose.

The more we give
The more we receive
The more beauty we unveil
The more beauty we reveal
Imagine everybody truly working together
Where unconditional love and peace prevail
No selfishness, greed, or judgment
The possibilities are infinite—
Anything is possible
Life is a precious gift—
Waiting to be unraveled
The world is a marvelous creation
With hidden treasures waiting to be discovered!

Chapter 8

Judgment

We are all equally different.

Judgment is the act of forming an opinion about someone or something that sets a precedent with the potential to spiral limitlessly. The judgments we make and the opinions we form about ourselves and others can tell us a lot about the relationships we have with both ourselves and the world around us. Judgment is as old as mankind itself and can cascade for an eternity. Its impact is immense—devoid of empathy, compassion, kindness and, most significant of all, love. The act of judging tends to create separation between people, rather than bringing us closer together. We are all here on Earth to learn to love and accept ourselves and others completely and fully, without judgment.

Ultimately, we are all spirit, and interconnected in the intricate web of life. Each strand of the web depends on another for survival, providing strength and stability. If even one strand separates itself, it affects the entirety of the web.

Our spirit recognizes that we are all one, and seeks to reunite with its counterparts in order to live in peace and harmony. Our spirit does not have the same driving desires as our ego with respect to material pursuits and possessions. It has no judgment, and appreciates, on the deepest possible level, that we're all equally different. Therefore, we must walk our own path to true enlightenment. Spirit has a divine intelligence and thrives on performing loving and selfless acts without expectation. It appreciates that the more light we reveal in the world, the more beauty we uncover for all to enjoy.

When we love and accept ourselves completely and fully, we naturally love and accept others in the same way, without judgment. We see beyond façades and are able to identify with the natural spark of goodness or light that exists deep within ourselves and all other living things. This interconnects all life on our planet and beyond, and creates the ultimate state of oneness.

From this viewpoint, we understand that others are not superior or inferior; they've simply chosen to experience a different set of circumstances in order to realize their potential, depending on their stage of evolution. When we judge others, we deny the spiritual part of our being and our connection to all living things, lowering our vibration to the physical level of existence. When we do so, we separate ourselves from our spirit and allow our personal experiences, upbringing, and sociological conditioning to strongly influence how we view ourselves and assess others. We begin to view the world through our logical mind, narrowing our perspective and denying our spirit.

This limited perspective can often create unnecessary conflict in our lives and promote greater intolerance toward others. Our logical mind doesn't have the wisdom and divine intelligence of our spirit to see beyond the surface. It's important that we learn to appreciate and realize the impact of sociological conditioning and how our personal experiences, upbringing, and circumstances can have a detrimental effect on how we view the world and the way we choose to live.

Different customs and traditions help to highlight the impact our upbringing and conditioning may have on how we conduct ourselves and perceive others. For example, what may be considered polite in one culture may be considered rude or impolite in another. Some cultures may consider it impolite to look people in the eye, whereas others think it's rude *not* to look others in the eye. A person's intention may be honest and sincere, but the action or gesture may be misinterpreted, leading to an inaccurate judgment.

If we're going to create a more peaceful world, we need to learn to establish more harmonious relations and embrace our differences. We need to view others without judgment and appreciate our deeper connection to all living things. Ultimately, our true essence is the same, but each of us will have different interests, characteristics, personalities, and ways of doing things, depending on our state of spiritual development and the lessons we need to learn to allow us to fulfill our destiny.

There are no two people living on this planet who are exactly alike. Each one of us is unique. This is because every single one of us has our own unique purpose to fulfill on Earth and lessons to learn in order to live a spiritually awakened and empowered life.

Every one of us is given the necessary tools to positively contribute to the evolution of our planet. Naturally, we have different interests, capabilities, skills, gifts, personalities, and ways of doing things, depending on what we've come to Earth to do, and the lessons we need to learn to fulfill our divine life purpose.

Each soul has its own path to walk and lessons to learn, and as such, deserves respect for his or her role on Earth. What may be considered the right choice or way of doing things for one person may be the wrong choice or way of doing things for another. We cannot judge others by the choices they make, if we haven't walked in their shoes. All individuals are unique and special and have their own specific roles to play in the evolution of our planet.

We must celebrate and embrace our differences. After all, if we all dressed the same, and had the same interests and capabilities, we wouldn't be provided with the same opportunities and stimulation for growth and development. It is our differences that make us unique, providing us with the grand opportunity to learn from each other, as well as aiding our own personal exploration and self-discovery.

We experience ourselves through other people; we could not truly know ourselves otherwise. Everybody is different, and different people will very often provoke or stir a different reaction or response within us. For example, when we meet certain individuals, we may feel inspired and uplifted. In contrast, when we meet others, we may feel uninspired, drained, deflated, and perhaps even angry. It's important to realize that these varied reactions and responses to other people can ultimately teach us valuable things about ourselves, as well as the areas of our life that may need to be acknowledged and healed. They help us understand things about ourselves that may otherwise remain hidden or suppressed.

It's just like when we stand in front of a mirror. If we're happy and content with ourselves, the mirror usually reflects back a happy and content image. On the other hand, if we're unhappy with ourselves, the mirror will usually reflect *that* back. This gives us the opportunity, if we choose, to examine ourselves more closely and make the necessary changes until we're content with the reflected image. Without the aid of the mirror, we wouldn't know what we look like. Similarly, other people provide us with a unique opportunity to experience different aspects of ourselves that may otherwise stay hidden below the surface.

Sometimes particular individuals may arouse feelings and emotions that we've managed to comfortably hide or repress. We may not like what the other person reflects in us. Situations such as this often create a tendency to blame or attack the other person. It's often easier to fault others than look deeper within ourselves to establish the cause of our own reaction. This is the easy option, though, and doesn't serve our own personal growth and spiritual development.

Instead, we should look at ourselves to see what it is within us that causes this reaction to this other individual. If we don't acknowledge and, if necessary, heal what it is that's creating this reaction, it will continue to remain repressed, creating heaviness and leading to other problems in life.

It's just like when we try to avoid looking in the mirror because we don't like the reflected image. The image won't change until we learn to either accept ourselves fully and completely or change what it is about ourselves we don't like.

Sometimes the people who push our buttons and present us with the greatest challenges are our best teachers. They provide us with an opportunity to look deeper within ourselves and consider our own existence on a much deeper level—thus providing us with an excellent opportunity to experience, understand, and release those emotions, behaviors, attitudes, and beliefs that may be preventing us from experiencing our true nature.

We cannot always choose what life brings our way, but we *can* always choose how we deal with it. Too often we're very quick to find fault in others, without seeing our own shortcomings. There's no point in blaming others for who we are, how we feel, how we act, and what we create in life. This serves no real purpose and only gives our power away, making us vulnerable and more susceptible to negativity. It takes courage for us to look at ourselves honestly and take responsibility for who we are, what we think, how we act, and what we create.

As we begin to take greater responsibility for ourselves, the people, circumstances and situations we attract into our lives will also begin to change to reflect our progress. From this perspective, it's clear that the judgments we make about others are ultimately those we make about ourselves. When we judge, fault, or blame someone else for our own shortcomings, we show a lack of spiritual awareness and ultimately judge ourselves.

As we become more spiritually evolved and learn to live in the light of higher truth, we naturally become more understanding and compassionate human beings. How can we judge others and expect them to act in a way that their own lack of spiritual awareness prohibits? Furthermore, what does it say about *us* if we know better, yet continue to allow others to suffer as a result of their own misfortune or lack of spiritual awareness. If we want to attract more harmonious relationships, it's important that we reassess our relationship with ourselves and treat others the way *we* would like to be treated. Basically, we need to become more compassionate and understanding toward both ourselves and others. The way to do so is to learn to see beyond the superficial, and identify with the spark of goodness or light within all living things.

No person is intrinsically bad. Some people, however, for reasons we may not always be aware of, may do things that we do not agree with or understand. Being compassionate doesn't necessarily mean we have to accept or condone others' behavior. It's about realizing and accepting their inner essence. Essentially, everyone is good and has the ability to shine when given love, encouragement, and support.

When we unconditionally and sincerely bestow these gifts on others, we allow them to identify and reconnect with their own inner wellspring of love that exists deep within them. We also allow them to reawaken to the part of themselves that is all-loving and capable of achieving life-changing results, which could help transform their lives in truly remarkable ways.

A humble and compassionate person lives in the knowledge of spirit and constantly works to serve others without judgment and expectation. It is a natural desire of the spirit to want to help others realize their potential and offer unconditional love to all living things.

When we pierce through the illusion of separateness and view the world through the eyes of the spirit, we reconnect with that spiritual part of our being and the unity of all life. In this light, we can see that our consciousness is but a small fragment of a greater universal consciousness that interconnects all life on our planet and beyond. There is no separation here. We are all part of a greater universal consciousness that interconnects all life on our planet, creating the perfect state of oneness.

Our spirit has no judgment. It can see beyond façades and identify with the spark of goodness within all living things. It appreciates that we're all interconnected in the web of life, and everybody deserves respect for their role on Earth. Imagine if we all worked together, collectively, as a unit in order to support each other. The possibilities would be endless. No one individual can do everything, but together, we can achieve anything.

Let your light shine
And illuminate the world.

Let your light shine
And reach out to all the corners of the world.

Let your light shine
In all its splendor and brilliance

Let your light shine
And pierce through the illusion of separation

Let your light shine
And reconnect with the unity of all life

Let your light shine
And unleash your creative power and infinite potential

Let your light shine
And brighten our world!

Chapter 9

Responsibility

That which is reaped must be that which is sown.

Our modern world has much strife and is in disarray. We're currently going through a major shift in consciousness as part of our planetary evolution. Unfortunately, as human beings, over the many hundreds and thousands of years we've gradually separated our consciousness from the illuminating light deep within the core of our being, and have instead focused on the physical world in which we live. As a result, we've gradually lost touch with our true essence and have become lost in the allure of the modern world. This has created much division and separation among us, and is one of the major causes of the chaos and confusion we're currently experiencing.

Being a part of this chaotic and confusing process can sometimes be discouraging and overwhelming, but as always, we have a choice. We can choose to either live in denial and do nothing; or we can choose to reawaken to our innate power and potential, consciously choosing to create the positive change that is much needed in our world today.

If we're going to effect real change, first and foremost we must acknowledge the spiritual part of our being and start to take a greater responsibility for our role in the creation process and the choices we make. Ultimately, we are spirit, and come to the Earth plane–level of existence to rediscover and live this simple truth. As spiritual beings, we have incredible power, and the potential to change not only our own lives, but the world in which we live. The power of the spirit is huge, and has the ability to transform anything and everything. Each and every one of us already possesses the power deep within our being to initiate and implement the necessary changes in our lives. The problem is, however, that in many cases, we're aware of what we need to do to achieve our goals and bring about radical transformation in our lives, but too often lack the motivation, confidence, strength, courage, and belief to take the necessary action. If we're going to change things in a positive way, we need to take greater responsibility for our life and the world we inhabit. We cannot always control what life sends our way, but we can control how we respond and deal with it.

With knowledge comes responsibility. This responsibility, however, can sometimes prove overwhelming, and the temptation to succumb to lower energies or simply withdraw or shy away becomes highly desirable. To turn away from our responsibility, however, denies us the power and privilege to create the life we truly desire and deserve. Taking responsibility means taking control of our life and not shifting blame onto others—that is, we need to become fully accountable for our actions and the choices we make.

We must stop playing the role of victim, blaming others for the situations and circumstances we create in our life. To blame others is to give our power away. We are creative beings by nature; and all the thoughts we think, words we speak, beliefs we hold, and choices we make will help determine what we attract and the quality of life we lead. It is, therefore, important that we start to become more consciously aware, and take responsibility for the thoughts we allow to dwell in our mind, the words we speak, the beliefs and attitudes we hold and support, and the choices we make.

We should not depend on external factors to provide us with the happiness and fulfillment we seek and desire. As long as we rely on factors outside ourselves, we will constantly be disappointed. Nothing in the external world is permanent; everything is in a constant state of flux. Real change comes from within, from the realization that we have a personal responsibility for our happiness and the world we create. If we don't make the necessary changes within ourselves, we cannot expect our life to change. The external world is a reflection of our internal world. When we find true happiness within ourselves, only then will we find true and lasting happiness outside ourselves.

For example, if we continue to think and act in the same way, we will continue to achieve the same results over and over again. We can't expect to evolve and reach new heights if we only repeat what we've done in the past. We must reclaim our power and take greater responsibility for the choices we make. With every choice, we either progress or regress. So, we should always consider which choices bring us closer to our true aspirations, and which ones take us farther away from our divine life purpose. In this way, our choices should be clear. Those that serve our highest good and the highest good of all concerned are the ones we need to make. Our choices should never be fueled by our own selfish needs or materialistic desires. Spiritual growth is the opposite of selfishness, greed, and separation, and means realizing our responsibility—not only to ourselves, but to all living things.

In order to overcome the many crises that threaten our society, it's important that we start to recognize and nurture our interconnectedness and learn to work together to create a new world. The key to doing so is to establish harmonious relationships with our fellow human beings, and learn to work together to help eradicate the doom and gloom that exists around us today. Collectively, we can create a better world, free from the suffering that is so prevalent.

The spirit grows through acceptance, kindness, and selfless service to others. If we perpetrate unkind and malicious acts and thoughts upon others, we cannot truly be free. When we open ourselves to love and light, we open the doors to our spirit, allowing it to freely filter through our consciousness and illuminate our world. The more in tune we become with our spirit, the more in tune we naturally become with others and the natural laws of the universe. As such, we can better understand and accept our fellow human beings for who they are. When we're in tune with the world around us, we can learn to live in harmony with it. We need to be able to relate to others and the world around us if we want to live in peace and harmony. The key to uplifting ourselves and those around us is to practice love, compassion, and acceptance, which leads to harmony in all areas of our life and the world around us.

Unconditional love is the greatest power in the universe and is truly capable of healing our planet. Since love is the opposite of hate, we simply have to allow love to flow through our being to truly experience its wonder. Love helps to instill within us a greater sense of hope and faith in our future. Love and hope provide us with the motivation and inspiration to strive for greater justice and peace and can change our lives forever. People with unconditionally loving hearts naturally radiate a true beauty that extends to others.

As we begin to make positive changes in our own life, we positively affect and inspire others to also make such changes in their life. When even one individual rekindles the light deep within his or her being, this person becomes a guiding luminous force, helping others to see more clearly and reconnect with the light deep within themselves. The more people who rekindle their light, the brighter the world becomes. We need to work together to save our planet from further destruction, suffering, and despair. We need to stop wars, violence, poverty, discrimination, and other self-destructive behaviors. These are all unpleasant situations and attitudes that create devastation and separation. They keep us in a perpetual state of division, hardship, and unhappiness.

Attaining spiritual enlightenment is the key to effecting a positive global transformation if we are to solve the problems of our world. We need to shift our focus and consciousness from one of separation, selfishness, and greed toward one of integration, unity, and compassion. We must learn to work together and take the necessary steps to create positive change. When we reconnect with our true essence, we shed light on our current global situation and crises. This needs to be a shared responsibility and commitment, as all of the problems of the world cannot be solved by one person. However, each and every one of us can make a positive difference, affecting the greater whole. Collectively, we have the power and resources to positively change our lives and the world.

Shooting stars
Falling from grace

Beautiful souls
Full of marvel and wonder

Innocent and pure
Precious and sincere

Akin to empty vessels waiting to be fulfilled
Delicate and fragile

Infinite possibilities
Incredible potential

Dependable and impressionable
Absorbent and compliant

Our responsibility and commitment

Capabilities abound
Anything possible!

Chapter 10

The Next Generation

*All the knowledge in the world is worth nothing
without wisdom.*

Children are precious and fragile, pure and innocent—
radiating divine light, natural beauty, and wonder. They have
a genuine curiosity about the world and an unquenchable
thirst for knowledge. They are generally fearless and
uninhibited, full of promise and potential. Their souls radiate
pure clarity and awareness, which is the nature of our true
essence and the closest example we have of the spirit.
Children are still untainted from living in the physical world,
just like empty vessels waiting to be filled. Children are
usually completely dependent on the people around them for
survival in the physical world, and rely heavily on others for
nourishment and support.

As adults, we often play a vital role in the spiritual, mental,
emotional, and physical development of young children. It is
our responsibility and obligation as adults, teachers, parents,

friends, neighbors, cousins, and older siblings to look after children and ensure that their needs are met.

Children usually grow and develop depending on the influences around them. They're highly receptive, and often unconsciously absorb and learn how to function in our physical world by imitating or copying those around them. From an early age, they start to unconsciously absorb the beliefs and attitudes of society, and the people closest to them. During these early stages of development, children start to cultivate their own individualistic character traits, often based entirely on their own personal influences and experiences of the world.

For all of us, these early years often leave a lasting impression on our soul and have a profound impact on our future, forming the foundation of our character and how we interpret and experience the world. The problem is, however, that as adults, we very often fail to recognize and respect the influence and impact we have on young children. Our kids need us to show them how to live effectively in the physical world, as they learn by modeling their behavior on ours. Therefore, it's important that we start to seriously consider our role and responsibility as exemplars, and how our behavior invariably affects how our children grow and develop.

Our current culture, which encompasses our educational system, does very little to foster the spiritual development of young children. Too often we simply teach them rules and regulations, deliver facts and impart knowledge, but fail to provide them with real opportunities to experience and explore their own inexhaustible well of creative energy and power. As a result, many children grow up unaware of their innate potential and creative power. If we want our world to change, we need to acknowledge children for who they really are.

When children are born, they're usually highly intuitive and powerful spiritual beings. As such, they tend to respond to energy as they feel it. They haven't yet learned to intellectualize it or hide their true feelings. Children tend to feel most comfortable with the truth and respond well to honesty. When our words and actions do not truly reflect what we're feeling, children will usually instantly pick up the discordance and react accordingly.

We must allow children to experience and express their feelings truthfully and honestly. If we do not, then they will begin to hide their feelings and lose touch with their spirit, as most of us have. This can have a detrimental effect on their well-being, as the expectations imposed upon them are often in conflict with their natural instincts. This can subsequently create unnecessary confusion, struggles, and discontent. If we acknowledge children as powerful and intuitive beings, we give them permission to remain true to themselves. Children need us to show them how to live up to their best potential in the physical world.

Children who grow up with poor foundations in early childhood can very often develop and display undesirable qualities and behaviors later in life. Unfortunately, as adults, we can often become intolerant with such children and tend to dismiss them as troublesome. We need to learn to be more compassionate to the needs of these kids. All children are intrinsically good, but sometimes, through no fault of their own, they can experience a lack of love, or worse still, be exposed to distressing and disturbing circumstances. They can become confused, and fail to understand how to lovingly receive from the adult world.

These children are often most in need of our love, support, kindness, and guidance. We need to address their underlying issues, harnessing the spiritual development of every child. Given their innocence, these kids are yet to absorb alternative ways of being, and can, therefore, not be fully accountable for their behavior. We can't expect children to behave in ways that they haven't been shown or haven't experienced.

For example, we can't expect kids to show love if they haven't been shown love themselves. It is our responsibility to give these children what they need so they can grow into healthy and loving individuals who can positively contribute to the evolution of our planet. If we don't give them the love and support they require in these early years of development, their problems and issues will just multiply. It is our responsibility, as adults, to encourage positive growth in children, which will ultimately lead to a productive and fulfilling adulthood.

No two children are exactly alike. Each child is unique and has his or her own path to walk and lessons to learn in order to evolve. What may be the right path for one person may not necessarily be the right one for another. Hence, we cannot expect all children to fit into a particular mold and follow a specific set of rules. All children respond and learn differently and require individual stimulation. What may be considered nurturing and fulfilling for one may be suffocating and unfulfilling for another. We need to consider the individual needs of children and provide a greater opportunity for them to explore and develop their full potential.

We should not impose our own acquired beliefs, expectations, fears, and desires on them, but rather, act as facilitators and help them uncover their own desires and potential. Too often we impose restrictions and narrow their imagination. If we want the world to change, we need to allow children to uninhibitedly tap in to their most inner and deepest resources from the core of their being.

Children are naturally curious and are learning all the time. We need to provide genuine opportunities for them to explore their natural instincts for growth. This will allow them to discover and develop personal areas of interests, and recognize their strengths and weaknesses, which might remain hidden otherwise.

Children should be encouraged to experiment and be provided with the opportunity and space to make mistakes. When we repress their natural curiosity, we impede their opportunities for growth, development, and mental stimulation, which cannot occur through repression. When we constantly tell kids how to act and behave, solve their problems for them, and make decisions on their behalf, we deprive them of valuable learning experiences. Life is about making choices and experiencing the consequences of our choices. In fact, the best way to learn something is usually through experience, which sometimes involves making mistakes. We need to allow kids to think for themselves and experience the effect of their choices. Understanding the cause-and-effect relationship regarding their choices enables children to take greater responsibility for, and control over, their lives.

Self-awareness is a state of being that allows us to become more fully aware and conscious of ourselves on a mental, physical, emotional, and spiritual level. By becoming more self-aware, kids are better able to understand and accept themselves; and are better equipped to change those things about themselves that limit their potential and stifle their spiritual progress.

Self-control is another important skill for all children to learn. It refers to their ability to have control over their actions. It also means that they'll be able to discern right from wrong, and eventually be able to make informed decisions and choices. Those who don't learn to do so on their own, but instead, rely on others, very often lack self-control and are easily influenced by those around them. These kids generally tend to blame others for their behavior and fail to take responsibility for the consequences of their actions. If children learn self-control from an early age, they're better equipped to make informed choices and potentially understand the consequences of their actions.

We need to encourage children to become strong and independent thinkers. They need to be given the opportunity to observe the world around them and draw their own conclusions.

In our media-driven society, children often become overstimulated, and can be disturbed by negative or false images and contradictory values. As adults, we need to teach them to base their opinions on their intuitive, spiritual nature and capabilities rather than only on what they hear and see. Children require positive guidance to think for themselves, thereby understanding the true essence of what goes on around them for themselves.

Children fundamentally have inquiring minds and should be encouraged to ask questions to develop a more flexible and open approach to thinking; consider, reflect, and analyze concepts; and look deep within themselves for the answers to life's problems. If kids simply accept and follow the old world order, we can't expect things to change in a positive way. The same old problems will merely be perpetuated.

We need to provide a safe and nurturing environment for children to freely express their ideas without fear of ridicule and judgment. Healthy self-esteem is of paramount importance so that kids can confidently share their ideas with the rest of the world. Children who have confidence in themselves and their abilities are more likely to act upon their natural instincts and share their ideas more freely with others. Positive self-esteem allows children to take risks and pursue their ideas.

It's important that children learn to have respect for the natural world that they're a natural part of. The world is our place of residency while in the physical form. Without the planet Earth, we would have nowhere to live. So, it is of paramount importance that we respect and look after our planet. If we don't do so, we will destroy it, and human life will fail to exist.

By teaching kids to appreciate nature and invest more time thinking about the environment, they will naturally develop a fuller appreciation and respect for life, as well as a greater sense of belonging.

Children represent our future generation and are capable of creating a far better world. They're full of potential and are capable of effecting real change. They are very clear and powerful channels who are highly intuitive and almost always completely honest. They tend to act spontaneously and respond to energy naturally. We can learn a great deal from children, so it's vital that we respect them and bestow upon them the kindness and unconditional love they desire and deserve. We need to encourage them to maintain a strong spiritual awareness throughout life and truly appreciate their magnificence. It's important that they appreciate that they're incredible beings with infinite potential. With this understanding, children can go forward and create a far better world filled with undreamed-of possibilities.

I am always at ease with myself
And the natural laws and rhythms of the universe!

Chapter 11

Dis-ease

Just as we can create dis-ease, disharmony, and imbalance in our life . . . we can also create ease, harmony, and balance.

A disease can be referred to as an illness, ailment, virus, syndrome, infection, or sickness. The signs or symptoms are usually recognizable, and at times may require intervention. Dis-ease is the opposite of ease. There are many external factors that can contribute to dis-ease, such as the environment, chemicals, pollution, and invading organisms. Dis-ease can also sometimes manifest itself as a spiritual challenge to help us evolve spiritually and learn to appreciate the true value of our health and the wonderful gift of life. However, for the purposes of this chapter, I'm going to discuss how we can often create dis-ease—on the mental, emotional, and physical levels of our being—through the mismanagement of our energy.

Everything has an energetic factor and requires a certain amount of energy to sustain it. For example, a computer requires adequate energy to operate, and if we cut off its energy supply, the computer may continue to work for a little while on reserves, but will eventually cease to function. Our body works in much the same way. Our biological system and cell tissue also require adequate energy to stay healthy and reproduce. Good health is achieved and maintained when the life-force energy within and around our body is balanced and flows freely. When the flow of universal life-force energy becomes unbalanced or disturbed in some way, then dis-ease and illness usually begin to take form. This can ultimately impact our health, happiness, and the way in which we conduct ourselves.

Universal life-force energy is all around us and within us. It is an infinite source of divine energy that sustains our world and flows through all living things. It flows through the physical body via seven main centers called *chakras*, and energy pathways called *meridians*. It also flows around us in a field of energy known as our *aura*. Life-force energy nourishes the organs and cells of the body, supporting them in their vital functions. Our mind and body are powered by this energy supply. The body depends on the flow of universal life-force energy flowing through us in order to stay alive and maintain health. It is the flow of this energy, within and around the body, that defines the quality of our health and well-being on all levels.

The natural and balanced flow of life-force energy within and around the body promotes optimal health and well-being. When the flow of this energy becomes disturbed, blocked, or restricted in some way, it is not able to flow freely and evenly through the energy pathways of the body. If we do nothing to correct these imbalances, eventually it will materialize into a physical symptom or problem. This is the body's way of informing us that something is wrong. It has been shown that wherever there is dis-ease, there's usually a corresponding blockage in the flow of energy to that part of the body.

We can disturb the natural flow of energy within and around the body in many different ways. Every move we make, thought we think, and word we speak requires a certain amount of energy to sustain and fulfill it. For the most part, we consume valuable energy when our beliefs, thoughts, and ideas about ourselves and the world around us are in conflict with our innate nature, denying us our infinite source of power.

The flow of energy within and around the body is strongly determined by what is going on in our mind. Our most dominant thoughts, beliefs, and attitudes about life will usually control the level of life-force energy we accept and allow to flow through us. The physical body has no conscious intelligence of its own. Upon physical death, when the life force departs the physical body, we become lifeless and incapable of functioning in the physical form. We are no longer susceptible to disorders and malfunctions of the body, and as a result, we see how the mind can strongly influence and impact our physical health and well-being.

When we hold positive thoughts and higher truths, we open ourselves to higher levels of universal life-force energy, allowing it to flow freely within and around us. When we accept or hold imperfect thoughts and false beliefs, either consciously or unconsciously, we restrict the natural flow of universal life-force energy. If we hold these negative beliefs and attitudes long enough, usually some part of the body will become unbalanced and suffer as a result (see Chapter 12: "Chakras").

We cannot separate our physical health from our emotional, mental, and spiritual well-being. All levels are interconnected and influence each other. Dis-ease in the body is usually the spirit's way of letting us know that something is wrong that we need to acknowledge and heal; therefore, it's important that we start to pay attention to our body and listen to what it's trying to tell us about our life.

It's vital to our overall health and well-being that we start to develop a more proactive attitude with respect to dis-ease and illness in the body. We can no longer simply assume the role of victim and do nothing. Instead, we need to view dis-ease as an important message from our spirit letting us know something isn't right, and take the appropriate action. The good news is that we can usually correct any imbalances by applying positive thought and action. The flow of life-force energy is highly responsive to our thoughts, beliefs, and attitudes. When we become more mindful of our thoughts and learn to recognize those that are restrictive or negative, we can replace them with more positive and expansive thoughts, which can nourish and support us.

In life, we always have a choice. We can choose to support thoughts, beliefs, and attitudes that either act to serve us or enslave us. By becoming more mindful and choosing positive and expansive thoughts, we can begin to open ourselves to higher levels of life-force energy. Universal life-force energy encourages and supports positive personal choices and growth, allowing us to make the necessary changes in our life. Universal life-force energy is limitless, creative, and has a healing quality. It has the potential and power to change anything and everything. By opening ourselves to higher levels of such energy, we can begin to transform our life and experience new and integrative ways of being. The result is that we can eliminate destructive thoughts and behaviors that tend to enslave us; and consciously choose to adopt more positive and expansive thoughts, attitudes, and beliefs that can promote and serve our highest good.

Chapter 12

The Chakras

To help us understand how we lose vital energy and how this loss ultimately affects our biological system, we need to consider the role and function of the seven main energy points in our body, also known as *chakras*. *Chakra* is a Sanskrit word meaning "wheel" or "vortex," and signifies one of the seven main energy points or stations in the body. These chakras are spinning wheels of energy; and help to transmit, assimilate, and regulate the flow of universal life-force energy in and around the body. The chakras are aligned in an ascending column, arranged vertically along the spinal column, starting at the base of the spine and ending at the crown or top of the head. Each of the chakras vibrates energy at a certain frequency, in a logical and orderly sequence. The heaviest vibration or longest wavelength is at the bottom, and the lightest or shortest wavelength is at the top.

Each chakra governs or represents different parts of the physical body and can be associated with different aspects of consciousness: an element, a particular musical note, a certain color, and other distinctive characteristics. The colors of the chakras are the same as those of the rainbow: red, orange, yellow, green, blue, indigo, and violet. It is said that our cosmic power, or *kundalini*, resides in a latent state within the base chakra. When this energy is awakened, it rises through each of the chakras, up through the crown chakra, located at the top of the head. When this power reaches the highest chakra, we attain union with absolute, universal consciousness. As a result, each of the chakras forms a ladder or stairway toward self-realization and enlightenment.

The first three chakras—the base, sacral, and solar plexus—are predominantly concerned with our external world and physical existence. They include all the acquired beliefs and ideas that we support in life. In contrast, the top three chakras—the throat, brow, and crown—are mostly concerned with the divine inner being and connect us with the higher intelligence or absolute consciousness of the universe. The heart, or middle chakra, acts like a bridge and connects our inner and external worlds. Ideally, the chakras must be balanced in order for us to be whole and complete, allowing us to experience the bliss of our purest and highest state of being. This is how we experience union with the divine, and self-realization. Unfortunately, in our modern world, this is usually not the case. Some chakras are understimulated, and to compensate for this, other chakras are overstimulated or overactive. The functioning of the chakras strongly depends on how we view ourselves and the world around us, as well as the decisions we make and how we respond to them.

The beliefs and thoughts we choose to hold and support will strongly influence the functioning of our chakras, and so, determine our state of being in the world. When we hold false or incomplete beliefs that deny our true desires, we create disruptions in the chakra associated with that part of our consciousness. When a chakra is unbalanced, the life-force energy becomes disturbed or blocked and cannot travel freely through that part of the body. If we do nothing to correct the imbalance, energy can begin to build up and eventually manifest itself in the physical part of the body associated with that chakra. While the chakras do not comprise any physical matter itself, they remain inextricably linked to the physical body.

The chakras engage with the physical body through the endocrine and nervous systems. Each chakra is linked with one of the seven endocrine glands, and also with a particular group of nerves known as a *plexus*. As such, each chakra can be associated with particular regions and particular functions of the body. When tension or conflict exists in a specific part of our consciousness, the tension is usually detected by the nerves of the plexus associated with that chakra. It ultimately affects the parts of the body controlled by that plexus, or the endocrine gland associated with that chakra. The health of the energetic system is, therefore, of paramount importance for the overall health and well-being of the physical body.

The physical body depends on the healthy flow of life-force energy. Our body, mind, and spirit are balanced and healthy when all of the chakras are clear and balanced. Disease and physical symptoms usually begin as ill conditions in the energetic system or body, which no longer remains free and clear in its energetic functioning. Imbalances in our energetic system usually stem from some type of conflict or tension in our consciousness. Understanding the chakras can give us important clues about our strengths and weaknesses; and the areas or aspects of our life that may need attention, improvement, or healing.

Understanding the chakras also allows us to appreciate the relationship between our mind and body. The effects of our feelings, thoughts, beliefs, habits, emotions, and motivations can all be found in the functioning of our chakras; hence, we can see our physical and emotional health as a reflection of our consciousness. Physical symptoms and dis-ease in our body can help us establish the location where we may be creating conflict or tension in parts of our consciousness. We can then consciously make the necessary changes to our thinking in order to correct these imbalances and encourage a return to a state of balance and harmony. It makes sense that if we've *created* the condition within our consciousness, we can also *correct* the condition within our consciousness.

The First, or Base Chakra

The first, base, or root chakra, known in Sanskrit as *Muladhara*, is located at the base of the spine. It is red in color and resonates to the musical note "C." The element associated with the base chakra is earth. Our relationship with our physical existence and external world often reflects our relationship with the parts of our consciousness associated with this chakra.

The base chakra is predominantly connected to our basic instinct for survival, protection, and security in the physical world. It deals with issues such as finances, home life, and occupation. The base chakra is also responsible for initiating new ideas and direction in life. Basically, the base chakra encompasses all the attitudes and beliefs we hold and support to form the foundation of our physical existence. The base chakra is also known as the root chakra, and enables us to connect to earth energies, just as the roots of a tree keep it strong and grounded.

When a tree is strong and rooted deep into the earth, it is self-reliant and naturally flourishes. It can usually withstand storms and conditions of any type. On the other hand, when a tree isn't deeply rooted, it's more susceptible to adverse conditions. Similarly, the root chakra reflects our ability to be grounded and present in the moment, allowing our inner being to be nourished and satisfied. When the base chakra's energy is deeply rooted, the entire energy chakra system that rises above is strong and powerful. Grounding ourselves enhances our ability to function effectively on a day-to-day basis, and to deal with life in an efficient and positive manner.

On a physical level, the base chakra is related to the skeletal system, kidneys, bladder, elimination system, sexual organs, and the lower physical parts of the body such as our hips, legs, feet, ankles, and lower back. The endocrine system associated with this chakra are the adrenal glands. The physical sense of smell (nose) is associated with the root chakra. Physical systems or dis-ease in these parts of the body are indicative of tensions held within these parts of our consciousness, which relate to the base chakra.

When we maintain and support constrictive or incomplete beliefs and ideas that deny our true desires and infinite source of creative power, we begin to create imbalances in the base chakra. If the root chakra is unbalanced, we may have a tendency to rely heavily on our external world for nourishment and fulfillment. If the root chakra is overstimulated, we may become highly materialistic, focusing on superficial pursuits and possessions. We may also have a tendency to be quite selfish and greedy.

An excess of root energy can be displayed as hyperactivity, inflammation, physical tension, inability to relax, anger, fear, mental and emotional confusion, rapid mood swings, an overpowering manner, impatience, fidgeting, intolerance, and even aggressive outbursts.

If the root chakra is understimulated, we may feel insecure, fearful, and anxious; and lack trust in the natural flow of life and in our ability to complete things. We may have a tendency to resist change, creating blockages on our journey to true enlightenment and fulfillment.

An underactive chakra can reveal itself through a lack of energy and stamina, a feeling of not belonging, and an inability to cope—not to mention congested conditions; difficulty with physical movement, coordination, and circulation; the inability to sustain energy levels; and physical weakness, exhaustion, and a lack of drive and enthusiasm.

Physical symptoms and traits potentially associated with an imbalance in the base chakra include weight loss or gain, an over- or underactive sex drive, weak immunity, anemia, depression, lethargy, an irritable bowel system, constipation, diarrhea, fatigue, exhaustion, cold fingers and toes, frequent urination, hypertension (high blood pressure), obesity, anorexia nervosa, kidney stones, and impotence. It can also create problems with physical movement, resulting in knee issues, strained ligaments, and pulled muscles.

If the base chakra is clear and balanced, we generally feel secure, stable, alive, optimistic, and strongly connected to our physical existence. We develop a deep sense of purpose and direction in life. We maintain beliefs and attitudes that nurture and nourish our spirit, and in doing so, utilize our energy wisely in order to fulfill our divine life purpose and follow our inner bliss. We feel connected to nature, with a deep understanding of its rhythms and patterns. We radiate physical vitality and strength, which helps bring about greater love, courage, stability, power, and growth.

Negative aspects related to the base chakra can make us fearful, anxious, ruthless, brutal, aggressive, domineering, resentful, self-pitying, obstinate, quick-tempered, unsure, and frustrated.

Positive aspects can make us feel courageous, pioneering, strong-willed, confident, energetic, determined, and spontaneous; and promote overall leadership qualities.

The Second, or Sacral Chakra

The second, sacral, or spleen chakra, known as *Swadhisthana* in Sanskrit, is located in the lower abdominal area, between the navel and the front of the pelvis, approximately two inches from the belly button in the area of the womb. Otherwise known as the "dwelling place of the self," it is orange in color and resonates to the musical note "D." The element associated with this chakra is water, which often reflects our relationship with the parts of our consciousness associated with the solar plexus.

The solar plexus deals with issues predominantly concerning sexuality, appetite, creativity, and intuition; and our relationship with power, control, and money in our external world. This chakra is also associated with the emotional body and our ability to engage with those feelings that allow us to experience our true desires. This chakra governs self-worth, self-respect, and our relationship with others. It connects us through feelings, desires, sensations, pleasure, and movement—enabling us the freedom to be ourselves and respect our own boundaries and needs. It also reflects our ability to relate to others in an open, honest, and positive manner.

On the physical level, the sacral chakra is related to the reproductive organs, excretory system, uterus, large bowel, prostate, sexual organs, lumbar plexus, endocrine glands, ovaries, and testes. The physical sense of taste—and therefore, the organ of the sense of taste, the mouth—is also associated with the sacral chakra. Physical symptoms and disease in the parts of the body related to this chakra indicate conflict in the parts of our consciousness associated with it.

Our spirit thrives on living honorably. When we use our power to control others and invest energy cultivating ideas that deny our true desires or support attitudes and beliefs that defy our spirit, we begin to create imbalances in the vital life-force energy going to this part of the body.

If the sacral chakra is overstimulated, we may tend to be overly emotional, sensitive, and sexual. If the sacral chakra is underactive, we may feel withdrawn, despondent, overly dependent on rules and regulations; and experience lifelessness, a lack of focus, feelings of inadequacy, and a disconnect with our emotions. There will also be very little desire or passion, and minimal or no interest in sexuality.

Physical symptoms and traits associated with an imbalance in the sacral chakra include infertility, ovarian cysts, endometriosis, ectopic pregnancy, testicular or prostate disease, menstrual difficulties, uterine fibroids, irritable bowel syndrome, impotence, water retention, digestive disorders, constipation, lower back pain; and problems with the uterus, bladder, or kidneys.

In its clear state, the sacral chakra encourages the free flow of information and creative ideas, the ability to embrace new adventures or change with ease, and a sense of purpose. Our emotions naturally flow freely, and we are able to express ourselves without being overly emotional. We have no problems dealing with our sexuality; and can be passionate, sociable, independent, and creative. Generally, we are in touch with our body requirements and respond accordingly.

Negative aspects relating to the second chakra include despondency, pride, exhibitionism, destructive attitudes, antisocial behavior, and difficulty interacting with others.

Positive aspects include joyousness, self-confidence, enthusiasm, imaginative thoughts, tolerance, patience, intuition, independence, and constructive and creative states of being.

The Third, or Solar Plexus Chakra

The third, or solar plexus chakra, known as *Manipura* in Sanskrit, is located approximately two inches below and central to the breastbone, behind the stomach. It is yellow in color and resonates to the musical note "E." The element associated with this chakra is fire; and corresponds to our relationship with the sun, often reflecting the parts of our consciousness associated with the solar plexus.

The third chakra deals with matters predominantly concerning personal power, freedom, intuition, integrity, self-control, emotional matters, and self-acceptance. This chakra is where our willpower comes from and is linked to our personality, ego, and intellect. It is also the center for psychic development and intuition, which can often be experienced as a "gut feeling." It motivates us to bring about positive change and use energy in a powerful and effective way.

On the physical level, parts of the body associated with this chakra include the stomach, gall bladder, spleen, liver, small and large intestines, the skin as a system; and the muscular, digestive, and immune systems. The endocrine gland associated with the solar plexus chakra is the pancreas. The physical sense associated with this chakra is the sense of sight—and therefore the organ of the sense of sight, our eyes—also corresponds to the solar plexus chakra. Physical symptoms or disease in the parts of the body controlled by the solar plexus chakra indicate a conflict in the parts of our consciousness related to this chakra.

Our spirit yearns to express itself freely. When we compromise our spirit in order to seek the approval of others, or because we fear failure or being criticized, we create imbalances in the vital life-force energy to this part of the body. We often start to conduct ourselves in a way that is in direct opposition to our spirit, and in doing so, we defeat our divine life purpose.

If the solar plexus is underactive, we may be passive and indecisive, overanalytical; and have a tendency to procrastinate, rather than trusting and acting on our intuition and gut instincts. We may feel tired, powerless, and withdrawn, and also develop a sense of self-victimization.

If the solar plexus is overactive, we may tend to be domineering, fussy, sarcastic, and aggressive; demonstrate a lack of tolerance; and fail to respect others' boundaries.

Physical symptoms and traits related to a solar plexus imbalance include poor digestion, weight issues, ulcers, diabetes, hypoglycemia, hyperglycemia, arthritis, pancreatitis, liver and kidney disorders, anorexia, bulimia, intestinal tumors, colon disease, stress, anxiety, the inability to resist infections, lack of interest or enthusiasm, food and additive intolerance, chemically induced allergies, impaired eyesight, liver disease, gallstones, panic attacks, headaches, tension, worry, confusion, chronic fatigue, arthritis, skin irritations, and peptic ulcers.

A well-functioning and balanced solar plexus brings us energy, efficiency, spontaneity, nondominating power, and control. It empowers us with a sense of personal confidence, self-worth, strength, the courage to embrace our true desires, and the ability to recognize and trust our intuition. We genuinely feel confident, alert, optimistic, and good-humored. From this center, we find the power and commitment to create and accomplish much in the physical world.

Negative aspects relating to the solar plexus chakra include vindictiveness, low self-esteem and self-worth, feelings of inferiority; and being overanalytical, pessimistic, cowardly, devious, angry, frustrated, confused, and depressed .

Positive aspects include being open-minded, good-humored, cheerful, confident, outgoing, expressive, wise, logical, and intellectual.

The Fourth, or Heart Chakra

The fourth, or heart chakra, known as *Anahata* in Sanskrit, is located in the center of the chest around the area of the heart. It is green in color and resonates to the musical note "F." The element associated with this chakra is air, and our relationship with it reflects the parts of our consciousness associated with the heart chakra.

The heart chakra is associated with that part of the consciousness relating to our ability to love ourselves and others, the ability to give and receive love freely, our relationships with people close to our heart, and our ability to discern between the heart and mind—which enables us to recognize and follow our heart's true desires. It is the place where unconditional love, compassion, and spirituality is centered. It is also the chakra connecting the body and mind with spirit; and is the bridge between the physical and the spiritual, the mind and the spirit. The heart chakra balances our internal reality with our outside world. It encourages forgiveness, compassion, kindness, trust, and equilibrium.

In the physical sense, parts of the body associated with this chakra include the heart and lungs, circulatory and cardiac systems, shoulders and upper back, breasts, and the entire chest area. The physical sense associated with the heart chakra is touch, and our sensitivity toward being touched. Physical symptoms or disease in the parts of the body controlled by this chakra often indicate conflict in the parts of our consciousness related to it.

When we deny our heart's true desires and our infinite

source of creative power to attain our desired reality, we give power to illusions of our mind, which can often create unnecessary fears and doubts, consuming valuable energy and hindering our ability to achieve our desired goals. Ultimately, they prevent us from freely acting upon our hearts' desires and taking the necessary steps to fulfill our dreams. When the heart chakra is imbalanced, we can begin to feel overwhelmed and trapped in life, affecting relationships with both ourselves and others.

When the heart chakra is overactive, we may have a tendency to suffocate others with love, and we many demonstrate selfish motives. People with an overactive heart chakra often demonstrate a lack of compassion, as well as jealousy and bitterness toward others. When the heart chakra is underactive, we may be cold and distant, insincere, lack self-worth, and be unable to give or receive love.

Physical symptoms and traits related to a heart-chakra imbalance include diseases of the immune system, chronic fatigue syndrome, asthma, high blood pressure, abnormal growths, insomnia, breast cancer, difficulty breathing, heart problems, chest pain, poor circulation, high or low blood pressure, and in more serious cases, heart attack.

If the heart chakra is balanced, it allows us to love deeply, feel compassion, see the good in everyone, and experience a deep sense of inner peace and calm. We are usually more friendly, cheerful, generous, empathetic, and tolerant toward others; and work on developing harmonious relationships. We're usually able to give and receive love with sincerity and a desire to nurture others.

Nurturing our spirit and embracing our heart's true desires helps us balance the energies of the heart chakra and can quickly restore life-force energy throughout the body. Unconditional love is the expression of the heart when balanced. This means honoring our spirit and our interconnection to all living things. It means creating for the good of all humankind, and being able to serve others without expectations. It empowers us to trust in the infinite power of the spirit to overcome all our adversities and tribulations.

Negative aspects relating to the heart chakra involve being unscrupulous with money, indifferent, jealous, miserable, possessive, inconsiderate, unstable, and suspicious.

Positive aspects include being generous, sympathetic, compassionate, understanding, harmonious, adaptable, unconditionally loving, and peaceful.

The Fifth, or Throat Chakra

The fifth, or throat chakra, known as *Vishuddha* in Sanskrit, is located at the base of the neck in the throat area. It is blue in color and resonates with the musical note "G." The element associated with this chakra is ether. The ether is the crossover between the physical and spiritual dimensions. A space where we connect with higher beings and physical reality is clearly seen and understood from a spiritual point of view. It relates to the space in which we occupy and create our reality. Our relationship to our physical reality or the things happening around us often represents the parts of our consciousness associated with this chakra.

The throat chakra deals with issues involving communication (both listening and speaking), creativity, self-belief, wisdom, truthfulness, clairaudience, and artistic self-expression. Expression can be in the form of clearly communicating our needs and requirements through words and actions; or may take on a more artistic expression such as painting, dancing, or music, which also enables us to bring to the outside that which lies within in a more creative way. This chakra is also associated with listening to our intuition and our ability to receive unconditionally, which is necessary to accept the abundance of the universe. This is the first level of consciousness in which we directly perceive another level of intelligence, and experience our interaction with it.

In the physical sense, parts of the body associated with this chakra include the throat, neck, mouth, teeth, neck, lungs, shoulders, arms, hands, and thyroid gland. It also corresponds to the bronchial or cervical plexus. The sense of hearing corresponds to the fifth chakra; therefore, our ears are also associated with it.

The energy to this part of the body becomes unbalanced when we suppress our true desires and do not openly voice our truth or emotions. Unexpressed emotions tend to constrict this energy center.

When the throat chakra is underactive, we may not speak our truth for fear of being judged or ridiculed, and we may have a tendency to be introverted. People with a lack of energy in the throat chakra tend to be shy and often keep to themselves.

If the chakra is overactive, we may tend to speak too much, act in a domineering way, and keep others at a distance. Usually, we're so busy expressing that we forget to listen. We may also have a tendency to be unfaithful, untrustworthy, inflexible, egotistical, and self-righteous.

Physical symptoms associated with a fifth-chakra imbalance include lumps in the throat, laryngitis, sore throat, tonsillitis, speech impediments, dental issues, jaw problems, sinusitis, chronic colds, skin irritations, inflammations, mouth ulcers, hearing or ear issues, chronic tiredness and depression, communication problems; and those relating to the thyroid, upper arms, neck, and shoulders. These symptoms are usually a sign that something is being held back or not being expressed.

When the throat chakra is balanced, we develop the ability and inner power to communicate our truth openly and creatively, without fear of ridicule or judgment. We become independent in thought and no longer feel the need to conform to mass sociological conditioning. We openly reveal our true desires, and trust our intuition to guide us. We're able to express ourselves in the most truthful manner; and are usually loyal, trustworthy, and tactful in our dealings with others. We generally feel happy, balanced, artistically inspired, and have good speaking and listening skills.

Negative aspects relating to the throat chakra include being unfaithful, untrustworthy, self-righteous, cold, domineering, introverted, shy, nervous, and inflexible.

Positive aspects include being loyal, tactful, trustworthy, peaceful, flexible, balanced, centered, truthful, and a good listener.

The Sixth, Third Eye, or Brow Chakra

The sixth, third eye, or brow chakra, also known as *Ajna* in Sanskrit, is located in the center of the forehead or brow area. It is indigo in color and resonates with the musical note of "A." The element associated with this chakra is inner sound, which is what we hear in our ears independent from events in the physical world.

The brow chakra is associated with a deep level of being or spirit, and acts as a mirror to our divine inner being. It deals mostly with mental issues concerning our imagination, creative visualization, meditation, and the wisdom that comes from direct perception or insight. The third eye is our intuitive level, bringing us information not necessarily available through other means. It is related to the act of seeing, hearing, and sensing—both physically and intuitively. It is the place where we store our memories, perceive our dreams, and imagine our future. It is the center for psychic insights and the foundation for these abilities. Through the power of the brow chakra, we can receive guidance and tune in to our higher self.

The brow chakra is the place where our true motivations can be discovered. It allows us to see things from a higher viewpoint, rather than purely for the satisfaction of the ego or our material comfort. It is from this point of view that we can see events and circumstances in the physical world as the manifestation and co-creation of consciousness, or human thinking and behavior. The brow chakra also relates to taking responsibility for our life, and being able to trust and follow our intuition.

In the physical sense, parts of the body associated with this chakra include our forehead, temples, eyes, face, nose, central nervous system, brain, lower head, and lymphatic and endocrine systems. The brow chakra is linked to both the pineal and pituitary glands, and is also associated with the carotid plexus and the nerves on each side of the face.

The brow chakra acts like a control center, where we decide how we view the world and manage our life, based on the beliefs and attitudes we choose to hold and support. When we deny our innate nature and divine creative power, we lower our vibration to the physical level of existence, allowing our external reality to dictate our state of being in the world and our motives in life. This dependency often creates conflict with our true desires and denies our inner creative power to attain our desired reality. When the brow chakra is stressed, the mind becomes clouded, and thought patterns may begin to function in a confusing manner. Our intuitive sensitivity may also become blocked, making practical decisions extremely difficult.

If the chakra is overactive, we may find it difficult to concentrate and develop a tendency to daydream. It can also cause headaches, confusion, fatigue, psychological problems, panic attacks, and depression.

If the chakra is underactive, we may be inflexible in our thinking and be less than effective in thinking for ourselves, relying heavily on external authorities for support and guidance. We may fear success and have a tendency to get confused easily, focusing on the intellect and science rather than trusting our intuition.

Physical symptoms relating to the sixth chakra include brain cysts, tumors, strokes, blindness, deafness, seizures, learning disabilities, spinal dysfunction, panic, depression, migraines, headaches, dizziness, nausea, and vertigo.

When the brow chakra is balanced, it empowers us with clear sight, allowing us to see the bigger picture and to gain a greater understanding of life. We develop a deeper awareness of our true nature and feel strongly connected to the universe, encouraging a greater sense of inner peace. We also become highly intuitive; and our mind is better able to receive, recognize, and interpret the divine guidance and inspiration coming from the spirit. This enables us to separate reality from fantasy or delusion. We generally feel that we're in control of our lives and have the courage to follow our inner bliss without being easily influenced or distracted by external factors or the materialistic allure of the modern world.

Negative aspects related to the brow chakra include feeling separate, fearful, intolerant, impractical, judgmental, inconsiderate, depressed, overanalytical, and having a lack of clarity.

Positive aspects include having a high degree of intuition, fidelity, unity, fearlessness, devotion to duty, articulateness, practical idealism, and an elevated state of consciousness.

The Seventh, or Crown Chakra

The seventh, or crown chakra, known as *Sahasrara* in Sanskrit, is located at the crown of the head. It is purple or violet in color and resonates with the musical note "B." The element associated with this chakra is white or divine light. This is what we experience when we're in the deepest part of our being as a point of consciousness, glowing in intelligence and brilliance. It is the most subtle element from which all things are created, traveling at speeds beyond comprehension, allowing us to be everywhere at once, and yet without having any distinct or tangible point of reference. The crown chakra connects us to the bigger picture and beyond—a timeless space, a matrix that is all-knowing—enabling us to communicate and link up with spirit.

The crown chakra is oriented toward self-realization and enlightenment, dealing with issues concerning our spiritual development and growth; and our sense of empathy, unity, and spiritual awareness. This is the chakra associated with thoughts, consciousness, wisdom, and information from the subtle dimensions or spiritual energy. It is the gateway to cosmic consciousness or higher intelligence. In much the same way that the base chakra connects us firmly and securely to the earth, the crown chakra opens us up to the universal energy of cosmic consciousness. The crown chakra relates to consciousness as pure awareness. This chakra is all-knowing—just as the other chakras relate to seeing, doing, or feeling. It is through the crown chakra that we receive information and inspired ideas. We then tend to run our ideas through the lower chakras before we bring them into manifestation.

This chakra is often depicted by a lotus flower, symbolic of purity, due to the grace and ability to rise above muddy, murky waters in order to achieve spiritual enlightenment and awakening. The crown chakra oversees and channels universal life-force energy within, maintaining essential balance in its entirety.

In the physical sense, the parts of the body associated with this chakra include the top of the head, the brain, and the entire nervous system. It physically influences the cerebral cortex, cerebrum, pineal and pituitary glands, and the hormones related to them.

If the crown chakra is underactive, it can result in a sense of isolation and not belonging caused by our lack of connection to the vital life force. This may result from a feeling of depression, a constant sense of frustration, and emotions being misunderstood. We may have very little concern for others, lack spiritual awareness, and can harbor a sense of narrow-mindedness. We may also have an overall lack of interest and motivation in life, feeling inert and prone to boredom.

If the crown chakra is overstimulated, we may develop a tendency to over-intellectualize and become addicted to spirituality, neglecting our physical needs. It can also lead to dreaminess, being impractical, and feeling disconnected from reality. This can usually be easily resolved by grounding oneself at the root chakra.

Some of the associated problems or symptoms relating to the crown chakra include immune disorders, migraines, headaches, depression, Parkinson's disease, schizophrenia, epilepsy, senile dementia, Alzheimer's, confusion, dizziness, sleep deprivation, panic attacks, anxiety, stress, an inability to learn, and other mental disorders.

If the crown chakra is balanced, it brings about knowledge, wisdom, understanding, and spiritual awareness. We naturally develop a greater understanding of life and are better equipped to fulfill our divine life purpose. This naturally instills in us a greater sense of contentment and fulfillment. It allows us to embrace change with ease, recognize and interpret divine guidance, and trust our intuition. We're released from ego-driven desires and are better able to trust in the natural flow of life—taking us where we need to be in the right order and time. We know that we're constantly being guided by a higher force or intelligence.

Negative aspects relating to the crown chakra include depression, confusion, mental disorders, a lack of concern for others, loneliness, feelings of superiority, narrow-mindedness, a disconnect with reality, negative thinking, low self-esteem, a misuse of power, and a lack of faith or belief.

Positive aspects include self-knowledge, spiritual awareness, devotion, dedication, a reverence for all life, a high level of intuition, the development of psychic abilities, spiritual growth, and deeper understanding.

Bathe in the magical sunlight
and allow its healing rays to illuminate your life!

Chapter 13

Color

Color is an integral part of our life and can help enrich every aspect of our being.

We live in a colorful world, and throughout our life we're naturally surrounded and exposed to color every day, in every way. Color is an integral part of our life, even though sometimes we take it for granted. It's impossible to escape the energy vibrations given off by different colors. Color can be found everywhere and anywhere, as it is an aspect of everything that we do and engage with.

The clothes we wear, the cars we drive, the public transportation system we use, the foods we eat, the natural wonders around us—all are rich in color. It affects every environment: our homes, workplaces, academic and medical institutions, and so much more. Color is a powerful source of energy and can have a profound effect on us at all levels: physical, mental, emotional, and spiritual.

The influence of color varies within cultures as well as within individuals. While it's a nonverbal form of communication, it speaks volumes to those with the knowledge and understanding of its meaning. Color is interchangeable and nonstatic; it can change from day to day depending on our level of engagement with our energy, spiritual self, and emotional well-being. By learning how color influences and affects us, we can begin to use it effectively to help restore balance and harmony in our life.

Color is essentially energy. Our most important source of energy is light, as the entire spectrum of color is derived from it. Our main source of light on this planet is the sun. We naturally respond to this light and are fueled by the energy of sunlight. It is a natural prerequisite for life and growth on our planet. A lack of sunlight can cause a lack of energy, and even depression. Light is an essential source of energy that we can often see in the form of color. The seven color rays that emanate from light possess different energy vibrations and wavelengths. Isaac Newton proved this when he passed a beam of light through a glass prism, whereupon it split into particles and revealed the colors of the rainbow. Color is simply light of different wavelengths and frequencies. Each color of the spectrum has its own properties depending on its wavelength and frequency.

At the lower end of the spectrum, red has a higher wavelength and lower frequency, whereas purple or violet at the top end of the spectrum has a lower wavelength and higher frequency. We're naturally influenced and affected by the distinctive vibrations that each color possesses. The invisible vibrations of color can either relax or stimulate us, depending on the color. Generally, red, orange, and yellow are warm and energizing. They give off a feeling of energy, excitement, and joy. Blue, indigo, and purple are cooler and more calming. They help quiet the mind and so, aid relaxation. Each color of the spectrum vibrates at its own rate and resonates with energies in different areas of the body.

The invisible spectrum of color consists of the seven energies of the rainbow: red, orange, yellow, green, blue, indigo, and violet, which correspond to the seven main chakras of the body. Each color is unique and has its own specific energy or life-enhancing quality, according to its wavelength and vibration. These vibrations correspond to our body's inner vibrations, influencing the flow and balance of our energy system. Each part of the body resonates to different colors and will affect us emotionally, physically, mentally, and spiritually (see Chapter 12: "Chakras"). To maintain good health, we need the energy from all colors of the spectrum. The healthy use of color can help enhance and stimulate the natural flow of energy within the body. The misuse of color can have an undesired effect and create imbalances in the natural flow of energy.

By understanding the language and impact of color, we can learn to use it effectively in our everyday life. We all generally have different color preferences. These color choices can reveal a great deal of information about ourselves and how we may be feeling. Also, it can indicate where there may be an imbalance of color. This will help identify potential issues that may need to be acknowledged and healed.

When we're well, we may be impartial to color. Imbalances, on the other hand, will tend to bring out preferences to different colors, as they can often reflect and support our feelings, and in particular, our personality. Spontaneous selection can often indicate what we need at that particular moment. For example, red may be selected if we require an energy boost, orange for creativity and inspiration, and so on. Aversion to a particular color may indicate an imbalance in a particular area of the body that may require healing and attention. The correct use of color is an effective way to harmonize our own inner vibrations and help restore equilibrium, balance, and harmony.

Knowledge, understanding, and effective use of color can provide an inspirational journey toward self-discovery and exploration. It has a profound effect on the conscious and subconscious mind; and can enrich, empower, and inspire us on a daily basis. Below is a brief description of the attributes of the seven colors of the visible spectrum; and how they can be used to enhance the quality of our life on all levels: mental, physical, emotional, and spiritual.

Red

The color red is full of power and passion and connects us to our physical body. It is the color of life and is charged with energy, vitality, courage, and determination. It creates warmth and excitement; and is lively, stimulating, and energizing. Red commands attention, stimulates movement, and initiates action. It helps build confidence and willpower. When red is managed well within the system, its energy can be used to motivate people and promote a greater interest and enthusiasm for life. The base or root chakra (Muldhara) is related to red. The complementary color to red is blue.

Red is a powerful color and can be used to help strengthen the body and aid in our recovery from illness. Primarily, red is associated with the reproductive organs and blood circulation. It can create life through its sexual energy, awaken our physical life force, and ignite passion and stimulation within us. Red can be used to overcome depression and encourage a renewed interest in life. It enhances human metabolism and circulation and increases respiration rates and body temperature; furthermore, it can stimulate the appetite. Red can also be used to relieve colds, chills, fatigue, or exhaustion; and relieve joint or muscle stiffness.

Excessive exposure to the red ray can often produce undesired effects and consequences. It can overstimulate the nerves, creating unnecessary anxiety, restlessness, and irritability. It can result in self-centeredness and ruthlessness, causing people to focus on their own needs at the expense of others. It may generate a misuse of power in the form of oppressive and cruel behavior for personal gain and advantage. At worst, red in excess can lead to aggression, violence, and other types of destructive behavior.

Positive Aspects:

Courage, a pioneering spirit, leadership, willpower, confidence, energy, determination, spontaneity, stimulation, excitement, assertiveness, passion, power, strength

Negative Aspects:

Fear of progress, ruthlessness, brutality, aggression, dominance, resentment, self-pity, inflexibility, quick-temperedness, defiance, conflict, danger, restlessness, agitation, violence, destructive behavior

Orange

The orange ray is a combination of fiery red and bright, sunny yellow. The red helps to reenergize the body, and the yellow helps stimulate and focus the mind. Orange is a dynamic energy like red; however, it is more thoughtful and controlled. It tends to stimulate in a more gentle way and is less explosive and aggressive than red. Orange represents enthusiasm, exploration, creativity, determination, encouragement, and stimulation. It is also a powerful emotional stimulant, serving to uncover and remove inhibitions and repressed emotions. It provides the confidence and courage to trust our intuition and freely explore our creative impulses. The sacral chakra (Svadhisthana) is related to orange. The complementary color to orange is indigo.

Orange can help relieve boredom and instill a renewed interest and motivation in life. Primarily, orange is linked to the lower back, lower intestines, kidneys, adrenal glands, and abdomen. It can help enhance immunity and improve all digestive ailments. Orange can be used to treat asthma, bronchitis, epilepsy, mental disorders, rheumatism, torn ligaments, broken bones, and muscular pain. It can also help bring about understanding and comfort in times of grief, loss, and bereavement. Orange is emotionally uplifting and useful for alleviating depression, loneliness, sexually related issues, emotional repression, and tiredness. Additionally, it helps to remove inhibitions and fears, and provides the strength and courage to move forward with a sense of ease and excitement. Orange is particularly beneficial to young people, providing fun, sociability, enthusiasm, and motivation. It also aids mental and physical stimulation.

Excessive orange can lead to the exact opposite, including deprivation, withdrawal, and seclusion. It can also encourage frivolity; a lack of seriousness; extroverted, uninhibited behavior; exhibitionism; and showing off.

Positive Aspects:

Joy, self-confidence, enthusiasm, independence, sociability, constructiveness, creativity, warmth, security, sensuality, passion, abundance, fun, happiness, energy, self-assurance, adventure, optimism, charm, kindness, generosity, encouragement, endurance, persistence, friendliness, purpose, bravery, self-reliance, resourcefulness, and tolerance

Negative Aspects:

Despondency, pride, exhibitionism, dependency, destructive attitudes, unsociability, deprivation, frustration, frivolity, immaturity, arrogance, depression, dominance, free-loading tendencies, deception, vanity, and indolence

Yellow

Yellow is the color of sunshine. It encourages a feeling of well-being and optimism. It is a warm color and essentially has a stimulating effect. Yellow is associated with the intellect, clarity of thought, joy, and happiness. It is full of creative and intellectual energy and serves particularly well during times of study. It is closely related to knowledge; therefore, it resonates with the intellectual, logical side of the brain. The yellow ray helps to stimulate our sense of self-worth, self-esteem, and self-confidence. It also helps focus the mind, clear negative or scattered thought patterns, and stimulate a greater interest and curiosity in life. Yellow brings forward wisdom and helps us develop greater self-control. The chakra associated with yellow is the solar plexus (Manipura). The complementary color to yellow is violet.

Primarily, yellow is connected to the pancreas, solar plexus, liver, gall bladder, spleen, digestive system, stomach, skin, and nervous system. Yellow helps govern and monitor both the immune and digestive systems. It helps release toxins and stimulate the flow of gastric juices. Yellow is good for hormonal problems and helps evoke pleasant and cheerful feelings. It is also the color of the intellect, decision making, clarity, improved memory, and concentration. It can help with dermatitis and other skin-related conditions. Yellow is an energizer, and is a useful aid for relieving feelings of exhaustion, burnout, and depression.

Too much yellow can cause our self-esteem to plummet, giving rise to fear and anxiety. Excessive use can induce overactive or obsessive thinking, overjustification, or superficiality, with a tendency to change too often. Excessive exposure to the yellow ray can sometimes overstimulate, and induce impulsive behavior and overindulgence.

Positive Aspects:

Open-mindedness, good humor, confidence, wisdom, logic, intelligence, optimism, confidence, self-esteem, extraversion, emotional strength, friendliness, creativity, practicality, progressiveness, joy, success, mental clarity, changeability, knowledge, personal power, emotional and mental vitality, cheerfulness, curiosity, relaxation, freshness, tolerance, decisiveness, fairness, sharpness, honesty, awareness

Negative Aspects:

Vindictiveness, flattery-seeking tendencies, feelings of inferiority, over-analysis, pessimism, cowardice, deviousness, irrationality, fear, fragility, depression, anxiety, cynicism faithlessness, preoccupation, superficiality, hastiness, imprecision, criticism

Green

The color green is found at the center of the color spectrum. At this innermost position, it represents balance and harmony. Green is a combination of yellow and blue. The yellow ray conveys wisdom and clarity, while the blue ray encourages peace and tranquility. Green encompasses the powerful energies of nature, which represent growth, strength, and progress. As well as balance, green creates harmony and brings us back to our natural center, or core self. It connects us to feelings of love and compassion toward ourselves and others. Green symbolizes self-respect, self-reliance, harmony, and equilibrium between the heart and head. Green is idealistic, helpful, dependable, and diplomatic. It allows us to see both sides of the spectrum, bringing greater clarity and understanding into our life. Green suggests stability and endurance, and is the color usually favored by well-balanced people. Green is connected to the heart chakra (Anahata). The complementary color to green is magenta.

Primarily, green is connected to the chest, shoulders, lower lungs, thymus gland, and heart. Green helps cleanse and balance our energy, encouraging a feeling of renewed energy. It helps regulate and harmonize the blood pressure and nervous system. It helps reduce stress, purify the blood and lymph systems, improve vision, relax muscles, and soothe the nerves. It relaxes the heart, calming the whole physical and emotional body. It helps soothe headaches and is good for shock or fatigue. Green is also beneficial in cases of claustrophobia, as it helps to release the sensation of feeling trapped. Green also promotes peace of mind and encourages self-love and self-acceptance.

An excess of green may create an overaversion to conflict. It can keep us from embracing challenges that we may need in order to grow and evolve.

Positive Aspects:

Generous, healthy, sympathetic, compassionate, understanding, harmonious, practical, balanced, refreshing, unconditionally loving, restful, restorative, reassuring, environmentally aware, peaceful, self-controlled, adaptable, humble, peaceful, romantic, rejuvenated, abundant, prosperous, financially secure, soothing, fertile, home-loving, family oriented, humanistic, discreet, sensible, fruitful, benevolent, tolerant, talented, sympathetic, expansive

Negative Aspects:

Indifferent, jealous, possessive, inconsiderate, easily bored, stagnant, bland, suspicious, bitter, unmindful, greedy, undependable, disappointing, materialistic, envious, miserly, indifferent, fame-seeking, unscrupulous with money

Blue

Blue is the color of the sky and ocean. It is often associated with depth, vastness, and stability. Blue is the spirit of truth and higher intelligence. It symbolizes trust, loyalty, honesty, wisdom, and confidence. It is the color of communication and self-expression; and encourages us to freely communicate our needs, express ourselves creatively, and realize our potential. Blue affects us mentally, as opposed to the physical reaction we have to red. It has a cooling and calming effect on our senses and generates a feeling of peace, serenity, and tranquility. Blue is peace with a purpose; highly inventive; and the color usually favored by poets, writers, and philosophers. The throat chakra (Vissudha) is associated with blue. The complementary color to blue is red.

Primarily, blue is associated with the throat area, upper lungs, arms, and the base of the skull. The connected glands are the thyroid and parathyroid. Blue is useful when treating coughs, throat problems, teething, stiff necks, and ear infections. The blue ray is particularly useful in reducing a high fever and treating burns. It slows down the human metabolism, aids in mental relaxation, and produces a calming effect. Blue also opens the flow of communication and releases blocked energy. It has a pacifying effect on the nervous system and helps restore calm. Blue can help relieve insomnia, lower high blood pressure, calm the nerves, and soothe the entire being. It also has an anti-inflammatory effect on the body and helps relieve stings, itchiness, and rashes.

Excessive use of blue can bring about too much cooling energy, leaving us feeling cold, depressed, and sorrowful. Honesty is associated with blue; however, the reverse or negative side is allied with manipulation to a high degree.

Positive Aspects:

Loyal, tactful, trustworthy, peaceful, knowledgeable, healthy, decisive, intelligent, efficient, serene, dutiful, logical, composed, reflective, communicative, truthful, soothing, calming, wise, tranquil, peaceful, prophetic, protected during sleep, able to engage in astral projection

Negative Aspects:

Unfaithful, untrustworthy, self-righteous, cold, aloof, unemotional, unfriendly

Indigo

The indigo vibration heightens our sensitivity and spiritual awareness, while also maintaining integrity. Indigo is a profound and mysterious color, ideal for spiritual pursuits and divine knowledge and wisdom. Indigo symbolizes wisdom, self-mastery, mysticism, intuition, and spiritual realization. It is the color of profound insights and understanding. While blue can be fast, indigo is almost instantaneous; inspiration and ideas can seem to come out of the blue. The indigo energy connects us to our conscious self, and gives us the experience of being part of the greater whole. Indigo is the color of divine knowledge and higher consciousness. It strengthens intuition, imagination, and psychic powers; transmutes and purifies; and unravels the unknown. Indigo aspires to be a spiritual master, as it promotes justice and peace. Indigo is the color of inspired prophets and writers. It opens the subconscious, as well as the door to the mystical. The third eye or brow chakra (Ajna) is associated with indigo. The complementary color to indigo is orange.

Primarily, indigo is connected to the pituitary gland, bone structure, the lower brain, eyes, and sinuses. It can aid acute sinus problems, chest complaints, bronchitis, asthma, migraines, and sciatica. It also helps to bring down high blood pressure, control diarrhea, and is the best antidote for insomnia. It aids kidney complaints and helps disperse growths, tumors, and lumps of any kind. Emotionally, it can help cure deep hurt. Indigo helps rejuvenate the idealistic side in all of us; and governs the pineal gland, which controls sleep functions.

Indigo can have a negative effect when used during a depressed state, as it will deepen the mood. Blind devotion is also an indigo weakness that can lead us to become too obsessive.

Positive Aspects:

Highly intuitive, fearless, practical, idealistic, wise, truth-seeking, faithful, fearless, devoted to duty, articulate, discerning, organized, optimistic, tenacious, pure, compliant, spiritually evolved, intuitive, psychically adept

Negative Aspects:

Separated, detached, fearful, intolerant, impractical, judgmental, inconsiderate, easily depressed, immoderate, authoritarian, broken, submissive, puritanical, obsessed, false

Purple/Violet

Purple/violet is the combination of red and blue working together in harmony. Red vibrates dynamism, energy, and strength; whereas blue vibrates tranquility, spirituality, and integrity. Purple/violet is vibrant and energetic. It relates to spirituality and imagination. Both stimulating and inspirational, purple/violet enables us to get in touch with our deeper thoughts. Purple/violet appears as the final color in the visible light spectrum. It inspires unconditional and selfless love. It is the most subtle and unique of the colors, traveling at speeds beyond comprehension; and can be everywhere at once, yet has had no exact location. It is mysterious and magical; absent of ego and aspired to by poets, psychics, writers, philosophers, musicians, and artists.

The combination of red practicality and the unrestrained intelligence of blue gives way to an emergence of creative energy. Hence, purple/violet has a strong association with dreams, imagination, and inspiration. Purple/violet creates a balance between physical and spiritual energy, uniting the body and soul. It allows us to seek the meaning of life; and achieve higher consciousness, spiritual enlightenment, and fulfillment. Also, it is associated with psychic insight, inspiration, spirituality, and healing. Purple/violet energy is expansive and can permeate unknown regions far beyond current comprehension, which may encourage spiritual visionaries to enter into a fantasy world of unrealistic thoughts and wishes. If we can steer clear of this trap and avoid the lure and fantasy of the unknown, purple energy can bring spiritual calming for our emotions, healing, and enlightenment. Purple/violet can also encourage psychic awareness and ability, integrity, and humility—all of which is of immense benefit to ourselves and others.

Purple/violet has strong links and association with royalty, and is also known as the royal ray. It represents nobility, luxury, wealth, power, and ambition. Violet connects with the higher consciousness and highest level of thought. Purple/violet has the power of psychic perception and spiritual mastery. It is associated with richness, leadership, dignity, respect, magic, creativity, wisdom, and the unknown.

Purple/violet has unlimited universal access to new worlds and new dimensions; its power is immense. It is highly introspective and encourages meditation and deep contemplation—promoting, stability, compassion, sensitivity, harmony, mental balance, peace of mind, deep relaxation, and meditation. Purple/violet has the highest vibration and is viewed as spiritual and pure. It encourages us to develop our spirituality, seek answers, and aspire to our highest ideals for the greater good. It connects us to our spiritual self through creating a balance and union between the body and soul.

Primarily, purple/violet is connected to the crown chakra, which in its physical sense is associated with the brain and entire nervous system, the scalp, and the pineal gland. It is susceptible and sensitive to all forms of pollution; therefore, the immune system is vulnerable and at risk for allergies. Purple/violet is good for relieving stress, anxiety, and mental-health issues. It helps with addictions, insomnia, meditation, and spiritual development.

Positive Aspects:

Reverent (for all life), adept in profession, humanitarian, idealistic, self-sacrificing, kind, just, spiritually and psychically aware, authentic, truthful, visionary, inspirational, creative, mentally strong and powerful, mysterious, psychic, spiritual, perceptive, powerful, royal, transformative, meditative, stress- and anxiety-relieving

Also associated with: spiritual insight and renewal, psychic healing, balanced polarities, spiritual power, mysticism, astral projection, paranormal sensitivity, compassion, dignity, inspiration, wisdom, serenity, altruism, nobility, artistry, mysticism

Negative Aspects:

Feelings of superiority, power-mongering, no concern for others, lack of contact with reality, introversion, decadence, suppression, inferiority, mercilessness, spiritual haughtiness, self-importance

Chakra/Color Meditation

The following chakra meditation works through the entire chakra system, using color and energy to help clear and balance the chakras. Cleansing and balancing the chakras is very beneficial to body, mind, and spirit and is something that should be practiced regularly. Alternatively, if you want to focus on just one particular chakra, you can adapt the meditation to simply focus on that area of need, using the appropriate color.

1. To begin, lie or sit in a relaxed and comfortable position with your eyes closed.

2. Allow your body to relax, and focus your attention on your breath.

3. Establish a nice, gentle, and comfortable breathing rhythm.

4. As you inhale, fill your body with white healing light; and as you exhale, feel your body release any tension and stress.

5. To begin the meditation, move the focus of your attention to the root chakra located at the base of your spine. Allow this chakra to connect down into the earth. Visualize the color red as a glowing ball of light. Maintain your focus on the root chakra as you breathe the color red in and out of this center. Immerse your root chakra with the color red, nourishing and grounding you in the here-and-now. Imagine the color red radiating out from this center, getting stronger and brighter. Allow the energy of this color to cleanse your root chakra and heal it, releasing any negative energy, impurities, or blockages.

6. When you're ready, allow your awareness to move up to the navel chakra just below your belly button, and breathe into it. Maintain your focus on this area. Now

imagine the color orange as a glowing ball of light emanating from that location. Bathe your navel chakra with the color orange. Allow this color to cleanse this chakra and heal it, releasing any negative energy, impurities, or blockages.

7. When you're ready, move your attention to the solar plexus chakra, an inch or so above your belly button. Maintain your focus on this area, and breathe into the solar plexus chakra. Now imagine the color yellow radiating from that location. Bathe your solar plexus chakra with the color yellow. Feel your entire solar plexus chakra being filled with the healing energy and light of this color. Allow the yellow color to cleanse the chakra and heal it, releasing any negative energy, impurities, or blockages.

8. When you're ready, bring your awareness up to the center of your chest to your heart chakra, and breathe into it. Visualize the color green emanating from that location, and immerse your heart chakra in this color. Allow the color green to cleanse the chakra and heal it, releasing any negative energy, impurities, or blockages. Imagine love energy flowing in and out from your chest. Feel the peace as the green, vibrant energy floods in and out of your heart chakra.

9. When you're ready, move up your body to focus your attention on the throat chakra located in your neck area, and breathe into this chakra. Now imagine the color blue as a glowing ball of light. Feel your entire throat chakra being filled with the healing energy and light of the blue color, glowing and growing in brilliance, and clearing and freeing your throat chakra.

10. When you're ready, take your focus up to your third-eye chakra located in your forehead area. Focus your attention on the third-eye chakra. Feel your breath

moving in and out from this center. Now imagine the color indigo as a glowing ball of light emanating from this location. Immerse your third eye chakra in the color indigo. Feel your entire chakra being filled with the healing energy and light of indigo, soothing and bringing clarity. Feel yourself merging with the energy, and allow it to flow.

11. When you're ready, move up to the crown chakra located just above the top of your head. Imagine the color violet. Feel yourself merge with the healing energy and light of this color. Feel yourself merging with the energy, and allow it to flow. Feel your connection with the divine.

12. Your whole body is now filled with healing energy and light. You feel completely calm and relaxed. Repeat to yourself: *I am calm and relaxed, I am calm and relaxed.*

13. Stay with this deep, relaxing, and peaceful feeling for a few minutes.

14. When you're ready to bring things to a close, slowly start to bring your attention back to your breath, take a few long deep breaths; and in your own time, slowly start to open your eyes.

I radiate divine love and beauty
I am from the same essence from which all creation stems

I honor and respect myself
I honor and respect my truth

I am an incredible being of love and light
With infinite potential and endless possibilities

I open my heart, mind, and soul
To the incredible healing powers of the universe

I have the power to heal my life
I have the power to truly be magnificent

I am worthy and deserving
I am eternal and divine

I have the power to heal my life
I have the power to set myself free

I shed my cocoon and spread my wings
I am truly free to just simply be!

Chapter 14

Healing

Universal life-force energy is abundant, creative, and has a healing quality. It has the potential and power to change anything and everything.

Healing is a return to balance, harmony, and wholeness. It operates on the premise that as human beings, our innate nature is already perfect and whole. Unfortunately, however, in the world in which we live, we're sometimes bombarded by the demands of modern living, and we often lose touch with our innate nature. This can sometimes create disharmony; and have an adverse effect on our physical, mental, emotional, and spiritual well-being.

The role of healing is to restore the body, mind, and emotions to natural health by correcting imbalances and returning us to a state of balance and harmony. It's a wonderful process that allows us to reconnect with our most intrinsic nature and the higher power of the universe. Then, we can leave our troubles behind and move forward in the light of higher truth. There's something wonderfully soothing and uplifting about this process. It can truly transform our lives and bring about greater joy, clarity, strength, courage, peace, and tranquility in the midst of chaos. The most important step in the healing process is our *intention* to heal ourselves. Since everything is made up of energy, all healing ultimately involves working and engaging with this universal life force.

Healing simply involves drawing upon the healing power of universal life-force energy. As this energy channels and cascades through all living things, within its natural flow it restores the balance of energy throughout and around the body. Universal life-force energy surrounds us and is within us. In its abundance, it creates, sustains, and heals; and is an infinite source of divine energy that allows all of us to access our highest good.

Universal life-force energy has a superior intelligence and works at all levels, promoting physical, mental, emotional, and spiritual well-being. This vital energy is limitless and energizing. It is all-knowing, all-powerful, all-creative, and omnipresent. Healing is a process whereby we can consciously choose to activate, direct, and utilize this energy to correct and heal imbalances within the body, and in all aspects of our life.

We're surrounded by this energy, but like a radio station that is tuned in to the radio waves of a specific frequency, we simply need to learn to tune in to the correct frequency to truly experience its wonders. When we're not tuned in to the correct frequency of a radio station, the sound is often distorted and inaudible. The station does exist; we simply need to tune in to the correct wavelength in order to access its most powerful signal.

Accessing and tapping in to higher frequencies of divine energy works in much the same way. We just need to learn to calm our mind and raise our vibration to higher frequencies of energy. At first, this may require some practice and patience, but when we finally learn to tune in to these higher frequencies, we will be able to access these higher and pure levels of energy for our highest good.

As we learn to activate and tap in to this natural and abundant source of energy, we can draw upon its healing powers to set the healing process into motion. Universal life-force energy promotes healing by unblocking the energy pathways and correcting disturbances or imbalances in the natural and healthy flow of energy within and around the body. It promotes relaxation, clears blocks, and replaces depleted energy—restoring balance and encouraging the body's own healing abilities.

Universal life-force energy has a superior intelligence, and knows exactly where to go and what to do. Unlike conventional medicine, which often tends to mask symptoms, the universal life-force energy can go directly to the source of a problem. It seeks out the underlying cause as well as the presenting symptoms, which usually disappear when the cause is established and released. If we do not address the cause, it will usually materialize in some other form or shape in our life.

Drawing upon universal life-force energy helps open the energy pathways. It offers a deeper level of spiritual awareness by raising our personal vibration to higher frequencies of love and light. It also connects us to the superior intelligence and absolute consciousness of the universe. This helps us remember and become what we already are at the deepest level of our being.

When we reconnect with the hidden wellsprings of love and energy deep within our being—a place where an abundance of energy is stored and channeled—we naturally begin to experience a profound spiritual awakening and a shift in consciousness. This heightened awareness helps us recognize and release imperfections, which often create conflict and disharmony within our innate nature. It expands our mental, emotional, physical, and spiritual levels to higher frequencies. This creates rejuvenation and revitalization on all levels, and accelerates the body's own natural healing abilities.

As we become more aware of our divine inner being and power, we start to develop a deeper sense of our life purpose. We begin to pierce through the veil of illusion and reveal the truth of our unaltered state of being. We rediscover the magnanimous spirit within us, and the magnitude of power we already possess to miraculously transform and heal our life.

Ultimately, a healing takes place when we reconnect with our innate nature, which is already perfect and complete. It's comparable to a switch on a simple electrical circuit. In order for electrons to do their task in producing light, there must be a complete circuit. When the switch is off, a break is created in the circuit, preventing the electrons from flowing, resulting in the lightbulb failing to emit light. Alternatively, when the switch is turned on, it closes the gap, and the electricity is able to move freely, resulting in the lightbulb emitting light: that is, "a lightbulb moment."

Connecting with our inner essence or true nature works in much the same way and can be experienced as a moment of sudden inspiration, revelation, or clarity as the illuminating light of recognition shines on what may otherwise have remained hidden beyond the surface. These moments can be life altering and can occur spontaneously at any time throughout the day or night while we're engaged in our everyday business. They may come about through receiving a genuine smile from a friend or total stranger, walking in nature, waiting for a bus or riding our bike, hearing comforting or wise words from a friend, watching a beautiful sunset or sunrise, bathing in the magical light of the sun, reading an inspiring book, or viewing an uplifting movie. Fundamentally, these moments can encompass anything that touches our soul and allows us to experience or engage with our true essence. They may happen frequently or infrequently and may vary in intensity and duration. The key, however, is to try to maintain and strengthen this connection as part of our everyday life.

Healing is also something that we can consciously

encourage by working directly with energy. There are many things we can do to support and accelerate our own healing process and return to a state of balance and harmony. Just as we have the ability to create dis-ease, disharmony, and imbalance, we can also encourage ease, harmony, and balance.

We can support the healing process by maintaining a nutritional diet, healthy lifestyle, and by cultivating regular exercise practices such as yoga and meditation. Use of a variety of natural therapies is also a very effective way to encourage and accelerate healing.

From a psychological or mental perspective, in order to heal, we need to take responsibility for our own mental and emotional health. It's in our best interests to acknowledge and release habits, feelings, attitudes, patterns of behavior, thoughts, beliefs, work, and even individuals that create blocks to our healing process. Holding on to people and things that no longer serve us only ends up filling us with negativity. Also, this allows no room for the new or positive to enter.

Clearing these blocks cultivates a space for pure, new positive thoughts, beliefs, behaviors, and attitudes—all of which nurture and support who we really are and what we hope to become. The mind plays a vital role in the healing process, so taking responsibility for our thoughts, actions and behavior is absolutely essential. It is an empowering experience that subsequently allows us to exercise greater control over our life and the functioning of our mind.

The mind is the most active part of the body; and our thoughts, beliefs, and attitudes very often determine how we feel about ourselves and others, and what we attract into our life. If we don't learn to control our mind, it will inevitably control us. It is, therefore, vital that we realize that we're bigger than our mind. The mind is like a computer that we get to program. The trick is to step outside of it and observe what it is we're thinking or inputting at any given time. We can be sure that whenever we're feeling bad, we're usually thinking something negative or restrictive. At these times, we need to become more aware of our thoughts. This places us back in control. The key principle is to catch these negative and limiting thoughts, attitudes, and beliefs as they arise and replace them with higher truths and perfect thoughts that nurture and inspire us.

As we begin to nurture more positive and expansive thoughts, we will naturally start to feel better. Additionally, instead of focusing on what we *don't* have, we need to focus on what we *do* have. This helps create a surplus of positive energy. Feeling and expressing love and gratitude is the quickest way to reconnect with positive energy and attract more positivity into our life. Positive thinking is of paramount importance to the healing process. Where thought goes, energy always follows. Our thoughts and intentions help transform spiritual energy into physical energy.

Our thoughts are forms of energy and operate through the same creative power or life-force energy that sustains our world and flows through all living things. Therefore, how can we set any limit to its power—the same higher power that is responsible for all life on our planet and beyond? It is obviously a higher intelligence with infinite possibilities and endless potential, capable of achieving incredible results and truly transforming our life in wonderful and ingenious ways. If healing operates through the same creative power or life-force energy, we can see that there are no limits to our power to heal, other than our own choice to conceive something as possible. Therefore, it's clear that we're limited only by our own ability to conceive something as possible. We can attain anything we set our mind to, as miracles occur every day and in every way.

As we begin to heal ourselves, we will naturally engage in a process to heal others. We will begin to vibrate at a higher frequency, acting as a channel for pure life-force energy from the spiritual realms. This energy will flow though us and naturally radiate out to all those who connect with us. As a result, our soul will naturally start to radiate and glow with an aura of sincere love and compassion, benefiting all those whom we encounter on our path.

We will act as a divine source of light and inspiration, encouraging others to reconnect with their own inner wellspring of power and creative energy. When we exude happiness, we help others experience joy as well. It's impossible to give others what we do not already possess ourselves. The ability to heal others comes from our own personal journey of inner exploration, self-discovery, and spiritual understanding. Healing is limitless in its power, unconditional in its presence, pure in its essence . . . and allows us to experience ourselves in ways that may not otherwise be possible.

A soft and gentle voice
Uninhibited and sincere

Subtle and consistent
Gentle and persistent

Full of love and wisdom
Deep within the core of our being

A bright light glowing
Radiating in warmth
Shining in brilliance

A simple truth
A recognition we yearn and desire

A simple knowingness
Difficult to describe
Impossible to define

A gentle prodding
Difficult to ignore
Impossible to deny

Always speaking our highest truth
Always guiding our way forward

I am now free to follow my inner truth
And live the life of my dreams!

Chapter 15

Intuition

Deep within each of us resides a limitless source of inner guidance, wisdom, and higher intelligence that can be accessed through what is usually referred to as our intuition.

Intuition is the act or process of coming to direct knowledge without reason or inference. It is derived from the Latin world *intueri* which means "to look within," and can be recognized as a natural instinct or an instinctive knowingness that is understood without words or explanation. Intuition can be viewed as a built-in perception or empathetic response absent of reasoning, validation, or cognition. It is an act or faculty akin to premonitions, the sixth sense, or gut feelings. Our intuition acts through the same creative power that fuels our spirit and sustains our world. It can be experienced and recognized in many different ways and forms, and is how our spirit communicates to us and makes our heart's true desires known. Our intuition is always working, and can provide valuable insights into our life; and guidance on our path to true enlightenment, happiness, and fulfillment.

When we listen to our intuition, we connect with the wisdom and higher intelligence of our spirit. This is the part of us that is connected to the absolute consciousness of the universe that is all-knowing, all-powerful, all-perfect, and omnipresent. Our intuition is constantly working and can process information in an instant, providing immediate guidance. It is accomplished at lightning speed, whereas normally we would attain such a feeling after much deliberation and contemplation. Our intuition knows our true desires and motivations in life and always provides the best possible guidance for our utmost good. By learning to recognize, listen to, and act on our intuition, we allow it to become a powerful and unequivocal guiding force in our life. We all possess intuition; we're born with it. The problem is, however, that as we grow older and our rational mind develops and learns discernment, we tend to dismiss it or cast it aside. This can keep us from expressing our heart's true desires and living the life of our dreams.

Unfortunately, in our modern world, we tend to rely heavily on the rational and logical aspect of our mind and often dismiss the intuitive aspect of our nature. From an early age, we're generally conditioned to be logical and sensible, avoiding irrational and impulsive behavior. We're taught to suppress our spontaneous impulses and to simply follow expected and established rules of conduct. Generally, we're encouraged to look outside ourselves for guidance, relying heavily on rules and regulations, values, traditions, cultures, religion, mass sociological conditioning, and other external authorities to influence and determine our actions and motives. These early life experiences often create feelings of separation from our intuition.

When we consistently suppress or dismiss our intuitive impulses, we cast aside our power to make choices based on the higher power that resides deep within us. This suppression of power can ultimately cost us our happiness, preventing us from confidently following our inner bliss and creating the life of our dreams. If we continue to ignore our intuition and look for validation and approval from others, or make choices that are not in our highest interests, an inner conflict will usually arise. This is quite often the spirit's way of letting us know that something is wrong. In fact, it can be said that most of our problems in life usually occur from not paying attention to and following our intuition. By learning to acknowledge, listen to, and act on our intuition, we can begin to harness the full potential of our mind, bringing greater balance and harmony into our life.

We all possess intuition, but unless we develop our ability to use it, we usually begin to lose it. To aid in the development of our intuition, we need to first accept the higher intelligence operating in the universe that is usually channeled through our intuition and the wealth of wisdom that we already possess deep within. We need to make choices based on our heart's true desires, and prevent our rational mind from intervening in the process—creating unnecessary confusion, doubts, and fears.

In order to do this successfully, we need to become consciously aware of what is happening at the inner level of our being and the workings of our mind. This understanding will help us distinguish our intuition from the idle chitchat of our rational mind, enabling us to make clear and wise choices based on our heart's true desires. The more we learn to trust and follow our intuition, the easier it will become to see, interpret, and act upon it. Our intuition is always at work, communicating in many wonderful and ingenious ways, so it's important that we learn to recognize how our intuition communicates to us and informs us of our highest good.

Our intuition works continuously and waits patiently for our attention. The problem is, however, that most of us expect big flashing lights, loud sirens, and massive signposts with our names written all over them in big capital letters to pay attention. Unfortunately, this is not usually the case. In contrast, our intuition usually works on a much more subtle vibration. It can generally be experienced as a gut feeling or sensation, a sensing or knowingness without words or explanation, a deeper yearning for something more, a natural instinct, a spontaneous urge, a gentle prodding, or an inspired thought. It may also materialize in the form of symbols, hearing actual words, or seeing an image in our mind's eye. Our dreams may also reveal valuable information, as it's usually easier for our spirit to impart knowledge and leave an impression on our conscious mind when we're asleep and our mind is at rest.

Sometimes our intuition may communicate to us through other mediums within our external world. For example, we may be guided or drawn to read a specific book, watch a particular movie, or listen to music that may happen to inspire us. The right people, circumstances, and events may appear at the opportune time, providing us with the help, inspiration, support, and encouragement we need to make a decision or move forward in a positive way. We can also unravel and bring to the exterior that which lies deep within us through artistic and creative pursuits.

The spirit is a creative force, and naturally thrives on artistic/creative forms of expression. Projects and interests such as dancing, writing, painting, and drawing are all forms of self-expression that enable us to connect with ourselves at a deeper level and bring to the outside world that which lies within. It's important that we learn to pay attention to the gift of intuition and allow our spirit to express itself freely. The key is, when we have an inspired thought, a strong sense of something, or an intuitive urge, we have to try not to second-guess or question it. Rather, we should trust the instinct and act on it accordingly. If we don't follow our intuitive impulses, we restrict the flow of energy and dismiss the many wonderful ways in which our intuition helps to inspire and communicate with us.

We need to learn to trust, and act on, our intuition in order to experience real success in life. This, however, is often easier said than done, as following our intuition very often requires us to take a massive leap of faith into the unknown. Most of us like to be assured of where we're going and the probable outcome of our actions in advance. Our intuition, however, works in the moment and will very often only reveal the next step as opposed to the entire picture. It requires trust in the unknown, the ability to relinquish our need for control, and trusting in the power of the spirit to guide us and always create for our highest purpose.

The other problem is that when we first start to follow our intuition, we may begin to experience disruptions in our life; things may seem as though they're starting to fall apart. At this stage, many people start to panic and feel more comfortable reverting to old and known ways of doing things. The trick is not to succumb to the fear, or become discouraged if this occurs. This is usually a natural part of the process. To make way for the new, we first need to get rid of the old. These are usually positive signs that we may be releasing things that no longer serve us. We must remember throughout the process that what is lost is usually always replaced with something more meaningful and fulfilling.

For example, we may start to feel dissatisfaction and a lack of motivation at work. This may be our spirit's way of letting us know that the job we're currently doing has run its course, and it is time to move on. At this point, if we don't follow our intuition, we might allow our logical mind to get involved. This causes difficulty in distinguishing between our intuition and the many voices that speak to us in the form of people's opinions, ideas, expectations, sociological conditioning, and other deeply ingrained belief systems. These conflicting ideas may manifest as questions such as: "What if you don't get another job?" "How will you pay the mortgage and bills?" and "Will you be able to sustain your current standard of living?" If we allow them, these thoughts can become overwhelming, prevent us from taking the necessary steps forward, and stop us dead in our tracks. This is how so many people get stuck in mundane jobs for years and years that bring no real sense of purpose or fulfillment, subsequently leading to dissatisfaction with life as a whole.

If we don't act on our intuition, we will never truly

experience the wonderful joy, contentment, and freedom that is derived from living in our inner bliss. Instead, we will probably live in denial and never experience our full potential. We are on Earth to experience joy and use our creative power wisely to live the life we truly want and deserve.

When we follow our intuition, we stop making decisions with our head and begin to follow our heart's true desires. Doors will suddenly begin to open, whereas before they seemed closed. Life will naturally start to flow with greater ease, synchronicity, and joy. We will start to experience real and satisfying changes in our life. It's never too late to embrace our heart's true desires and live the life of our dreams, so it's important that we do what we love and love what we do. The universe will always conspire to make the right things happen in the right time when we're living our inner truth and bliss.

Life is full of wonderful and magical moments and opportunities; we just need to learn to recognize the signs, premonitions, and omens. Our intuition plays an integral part in guiding us toward our highest purpose in life, making our true desires known to us. It is the spirit's way of communicating to us and inspiring us. It is like a wise old teacher who is forever present, continually guiding us toward our highest truth.

By tapping in to our intuition, we can receive valuable guidance, insight, and clarity. Our intuition can provide us with an oasis of peace in the midst of chaos, courage and hope in times of darkness and despair, strength in times of weakness, and a genuine purpose when we lack motivation and lose interest. It's an incredibly useful resource, and a natural gift that we all possess, which can help us navigate our life and realize our dreams.

We all have the answers we seek deep within ourselves. When we follow our intuition, we increase the flow of energy and naturally feel more alive. Our intuition is never wrong, although sometimes our interpretation of it may be incorrect. Through practice, however, we will be better able to recognize and interpret our intuition. By learning to follow our gut feelings, we will begin to lead a more satisfying and fulfilling life, which not only serves our highest good, but also brings us into closer alignment with our divine purpose.

An expansive feeling of all-encompassing love, bliss, and peace—difficult to describe or encapsulate into words!

Chapter 16

Meditation

*Open your heart and let the light within shine in all its
brilliance, revealing your true desires and ultimate
state of being.*

Meditation is a process that enables us to transcend our
physical level of existence. It is an effective means of looking
into, and reconnecting with, our innermost self, at depths that
would not necessarily be achieved in other ways. Meditation
enables us to experience our innate nature; and inner source
of creative energy, power, and wisdom. It facilitates thought,
consideration, deliberation, contemplation, reflection, and
relaxation. The initial use of meditation is to help relax and
calm the mind, body, and emotions. The desired outcome is
to attain a level of higher consciousness that might not
otherwise be possible.

Meditation might be described as awareness of the mind in
its purest form. It can be practiced as a formal discipline, or it
can occur spontaneously throughout the day while we're
engaged in our everyday life. A state of relaxed attentiveness

is what is desired during meditation practice. It allows us to train the mind in such a way that we can experience increased happiness and fulfillment purely by exercising greater control over our thoughts and the functioning of our mind.

The human mind has two directions: internal and external. Unfortunately, given the demands of our modern world, many of us tend to spend most of our time focusing on the external world. We're predisposed to live in a state of perpetual motion, keeping ourselves constantly busy, affording very little time to benefit from the peace and stillness that only the internal world can provide. In fact, our consciousness is often so overinvolved with outside stimuli that very often we tend to lose sight of who we really are and what we need from life. This can often create conflict with our true desires, as well as a troublesome state of mind.

When we do not truly know ourselves, and our motives are in conflict with our spirit, more often than not we experience discord. A negative or scattered state of mind can waste valuable energy, leaving us feeling drained and more susceptible to negative influences. In a culture full of materialistic temptations and temporary illusions, it's important that we remain focused and not allow ourselves to become easily distracted or misguided by the allure of the modern world.

There are many things in life that are beyond our control. We can, however, learn to take greater responsibility and control of our mind. Meditation is an incredibly powerful and practical way of helping us do so. It is a mental discipline and practice that involves focusing our mind on just one thing. Our attention can be on anything, with our breath usually providing an excellent focal point, as it is easily accessible and present in our conscious awareness.

Through the practice of meditation, we seek to free ourselves from our constrictive identification with the external world. We allow our awareness to gradually gravitate toward a higher level of consciousness. This heightened awareness provides us with a unique opportunity to witness our life from the outside looking in, free from the distractions and limitations that often accompany our preoccupation with what's going on around us.

As we begin to focus our attention, our mind gradually begins to slow down. The more focused and aware we are, the slower our mind becomes, allowing the gaps between thoughts to gradually increase. The longer the gaps between thoughts, the quieter the mind, and the deeper we enter into meditation. And the deeper we enter into meditation, the deeper we delve into the center of our innermost being. This experience is empowering, as it provides us with a unique opportunity to observe our thoughts from a place of deep relaxation and peace.

Basically, during meditation, the mind becomes aware of itself. The moment we become aware of the functioning of the mind, we realize that we're not just purely "of mind." In retrospect, we realize that we are, in fact, something far greater and more profound. From this viewpoint, we can see exactly how our mind operates, allowing us to observe how our thoughts surface in an attempt to claim our attention. When we deny these thoughts, they gradually fade away, giving room for the next thought to surface. It is during this process that awareness becomes observation. Seeing the world through this viewpoint naturally changes our perspective. We're able to see the world as it really is; and having seen this, our rational mind, which is often fed by our external world, loses power over us and we regain a real sense of freedom and liberation.

Through regular and persistent meditation practice, turbulent, distracting thoughts will stop altogether. When this unrest subsides and our mind is silent, it's possible to meditate and focus on the soul, allowing us to experience the most intrinsic qualities of our true nature.

Silence has the innate ability to revive the inexhaustible wellspring of love and peace we all possess deep within us. These feelings, when invoked, naturally flow through our entire being and reach out far beyond, creating an expansive feeling of all-encompassing bliss. They help raise the vibrational frequencies of our body, and we come to experience the energetic part of our being: becoming light over matter. In this light, we're no longer disturbed by the incessant chatter and mental discomfort of our mind. We can step beyond our self-imposed limitations and the restrictive identification of our personal reality. As such, everything becomes clear and appears possible in the light of higher truth. Meditation feels like a wonderful return home, where nothing and no one can disturb our inner peace and calm.

While we're meditating, we rise above the concerns and worries of our everyday living and feel a wonderful sense of lightness, freedom, and liberation. The problem is, however, that very often, as soon as we finish meditating and return to daily life, we begin to lose the peaceful feeling and allow our external reality to affect us all over again.

The reason is that even though we've experienced a heightened state of consciousness, it has not yet become permanent. We cannot expect to change the habitual patterns of the mind so quickly. The mind is highly susceptible, predisposed, and easily disturbed. The slightest irritation in our external world is capable of affecting and changing the way we think and feel.

The good news, however, is that through the regular and persistent practice of meditation, our mind will gradually begin to slow down, affording us the ability to hold this higher state of consciousness and awareness for longer periods of time. But, it's important to remember that meditation is a discipline—not so much of *doing*, but more so of *being*. Initially, it can and should be practiced as a formal discipline, but in actuality, it needs to be something that we cultivate into our everyday life. This can be achieved by becoming more consciously aware of our thoughts throughout the day, and by taking greater control of those we allow to dwell in our mind. The key is to become more mindful in our everyday life and develop an all-encompassing meditative lifestyle.

136

Mindful living is a technique that helps keep us focused, and prevents us from becoming easily distracted and losing sight of what is really important to us. It involves continual awareness of the actions and interactions taking place in our body, mind, and emotions. By becoming more aware of what is happening within and around us, we can learn what disturbs our inner calm and peace, and start to take greater control of our life.

The key is for us to pause at various points throughout the day and check to see if we're in a mindful and attentive state of awareness. For example, are we relaxed and fully present in the moment, or has the mind wandered off somewhere else? If we find that we're not fully present, we need to remember that we have the power to control our mind and bring it back to the present.

By practicing meditation and mindful living, we become more consciously aware of the functioning of our mind and soon realize how little time we actually live fully in the present moment. For most of us, our thoughts are usually overpowered by our emotions, or are preoccupied with past or future events. As we become more aware of the patterns and habits of our mind, we can learn to change our way of thinking.

Mindful living provides us with a way to regularly clear out the mental debris, purifying our mind of negative and restrictive thought patterns that too often hold us back in life. Mindful living involves making conscious choices, such as choosing to be present in the moment and learning to control what we allow to come in to our mind, thoughts, body, and soul. We have the freedom and choice to control our thoughts and to live in a constant state of peace of mind, unaffected by what is happening around us. Through regular and persistent meditation and mindful living, we can begin to live life more fully and completely.

There are myriad benefits that can be achieved through regular and persistent meditation practice. It allows us to get in touch with ourselves on a much deeper level, and helps us remember who we really are and what we truly desire from life—giving us a real sense of purpose and direction. Regular and persistent practice leads to a state of consciousness that brings about greater peace and clarity. Developing a peaceful mind is of paramount importance to enjoying a peaceful life. And, a peaceful mind means that we're at peace with ourselves as well as the natural rhythms and laws of the universe. The more in tune we become with our spirit, the more peace and happiness we will find in ourselves and the world around us. Clarity of mind helps us gain a greater understanding of life and deal with difficult situations with greater ease, joy, and fulfillment.

Meditation helps us relate to the external world from the internal world, dramatically changing our perspective on things. This helps us cultivate a profound sense of what is right and wrong, instilling within us a real love of truth and purity of heart. It also helps us overcome our desires for materialistic and superficial things in our physical world by revealing them as insignificant in comparison to our greater need for truth, wholeness, and freedom. In stressful and difficult times, meditation is a particularly useful tool for relief and introspection, enabling us to separate truth from illusion, and so gain greater clarity. People who meditate regularly generally experience increased vitality, longevity, better health, and an enhanced quality of life overall.

To breathe is to live.
To breathe fully and completely
Is to live fully and completely!

Chapter 17

Breathing

Take the time to enjoy and cultivate every breath, because
without it, there is no life as we know it.

Breathing is essential for life, and is one of the most important bodily functions. The energy that sustains our physical existence and allows us to inhabit this planet is the breath. Life, in the physical form, begins when we inhale our first breath, and ends when we exhale our last one. Breathing is essential for survival and affects virtually every aspect of our existence. The human body requires oxygen in order to survive, is the most vital nutrient for our bodies; and is essential for our physical, mental, emotional, and spiritual well-being. We all know how to breathe; it's something that happens naturally and automatically. The problem is that most of us pay little or no attention to our breathing and have forgotten how to breathe fully and completely, which is what allows us to absorb the maximum amount of oxygen supplied by nature.

The increasing demands of modern-day life have caused many of us to subconsciously develop unhealthy breathing habits. Our quick pace and challenging lifestyle play major roles in the way we breathe. We tend to live in a state of perpetual motion, constantly striving to *be*, rather than just simply *being* and embracing the true beauty that surrounds us every day. In fact, we very rarely take the time to notice and appreciate the continuous flow of our breath and celebrate the magical gift of life.

We're often too busy—totally absorbed and engaged in our external reality. As a result, we become overburdened, and suffer from anxiety due to worry and uncertainty. Furthermore, we live in social conditions that are not always conducive to the health of our respiratory system. In many cases, we tend to assume slouched positions that diminish our lung capacity and restrict the flow of life-force energy. These negative emotional states and conditions invariably affect the rate of our breathing, causing it to be fast, shallow, and irregular—not just momentarily, but habitually. As we go through life, these modified and restrictive behaviors become a part of our everyday breathing patterns. If we do not consciously do something to correct these habits, we can suffer from permanent respiratory problems, which will ultimately impact other areas of our well-being.

Shallow and quick breathing can lead to a multitude of problems. When we inhale, we take in oxygen or life-force energy that sustains our existence and allows our body and mind to function. When we exhale, we release this life force, letting it carry with it any negative energy and impurities within the body. Shallow and quick breathing only permits small amounts of oxygen to be absorbed by the body, which is problematic since oxygen is essential for the production of energy. As a result, we often lack the vital life-force energy that sustains us and promotes our health, mental alertness, emotional well-being, and spiritual awareness. In order to live a more rewarding and fulfilling life, it's important that we learn to appreciate and cultivate our breath. It is this life force that sustains us and allows us to live on this planet. Without it we would fail to exist. Good health and vitality are achieved when this life force is balanced and allowed to flow freely. When it gets blocked in the body or we don't take in enough, our energy flow often becomes restricted in some way. These imbalances can often be experienced in the form of confusion, stress, dis-ease, and illness. In essence, learning to breathe fully and completely is a beneficial technique to practice and develop, as it can enhance every aspect of our life.

Practicing controlled and regulated breathing helps stimulate and balance the vital life-force energy that permeates our bodies and massages the internal organs. This helps regulate energy, remove impurities, clear and release blockages, increase vitality, soothe the nervous system, induce restful sleep, and enhance the overall quality of life. Deep breathing also helps raise the level of oxygen in the blood flow, and improves the delivery of nutrients to the cells. This, in turn, nourishes the organs and cells of the body, supporting them in their vital functions. We can also learn to control our state of mind and calm our emotions through controlled and regulated breathing.

Our state of mind is often reflected in the way we breathe. When we're agitated and anxious, our breath is usually shallow, rapid, and irregular. In contrast, when we're relaxed and at peace with ourselves and the world around us, our breathing usually becomes deeper, slower, and more regulated. The breath provides us with a simple and natural point of focus to aid relaxation and help calm the mind. Deep and controlled breathing is a particularly beneficial technique to use when we find ourselves in troublesome, frustrating situations, as it will promote a calmer response to life's challenges. It enables us to deal with our emotions more intelligently, and stimulates mental alertness. Conscious and controlled breathing can also help us go deep within ourselves, reconnecting us with the spiritual part of our nature.

The quickest and easiest way to draw our attention deep within ourselves is by reconnecting with our breath, which provides an unbroken link or bridge from the known to the unknown—matter to energy, physical to spiritual, conscious to unconscious—connecting and balancing the two hemispheres of the brain. The breath connects us to each other and everything in the universe. It is always available to receive our conscious awareness, providing an easily accessible point of focus. This helps calm our mind and connect us to ourselves on a much deeper level. Breathing helps to keep us grounded within our body, while also keeping us present in the moment. It is the quickest way to regain our composure in difficult or challenging situations, enabling us to remain focused and centered.

The importance of breathing techniques that have the capacity to transform our lives is often underestimated. Breathing is the most important bodily function and provides us with a strong link between body, mind, and spirit. The correct use of breathing techniques is an excellent tool for reducing stress and promoting relaxation. Breathing in an efficient manner also maintains a natural flow and movement of energy within the body; and positively affects our mental, emotional, physical, and spiritual well-being. This, naturally, enhances our overall health and greatly improves every aspect of our life.

Breathing Exercise

There are many different types of breathing exercises available. For more advanced techniques, it's best to consult books or classes specifically dedicated to such practices, or to consult an expert in the area.

Following is a simple breathing exercise that will allow you to quickly connect with the vitality and spark of divine energy deep within your soul, promoting greater inner peace, spiritual awareness, and tranquility.

1. Begin by lying flat on your back. Make sure no part of your body is strained or supporting weight. Or, you can stand, or sit up in a chair. The spine should be kept straight so as not to restrict the flow of energy, and ideally, palms should be facing upward.

2. Relax your jaw, and let your tongue drop away from the roof of your mouth.

3. Place one hand on your stomach just above your navel, and the other hand just below your breastbone or sternum.

4. Close your eyes and focus your attention on your breath and abdominal area. Be aware of the gentle inflow and outflow of air in your body.

5. Slowly and smoothly inhale through your nose, keeping your mouth closed. Feel your abdomen rising and inflating, then your rib cage, and be conscious of the air filling your upper chest area.

6. Slowly and smoothly exhale through your nose, keeping your mouth closed. Relax your chest and ribs—the air will expel naturally. Finally, when all the air seems to be out, push your stomach in slightly to release any

remaining air in your lungs. Gently feel your belly sinking back toward your spine.

7. Repeat Steps 5 and 6 in smooth succession for five minutes, or until your breathing rate has slowed and you feel calm and peaceful. Feel your body expanding with the inhalation, and contracting with the exhalation.

8. When you're ready, resume regular breathing.

Things to Note

• Ensure that the transition between your breaths is smooth and regular. Inhalation and exhalation is performed in one smooth, continual flow. Inhalation is done from the bottom up, and exhalation from the top down. No effort or strain should be exerted. There should be a gradual increase in the duration of time during your breathing practice.

• It's important to breathe in as well as out through the nose. By breathing through the nose, you will feel your diaphragm expand, rather than your chest, allowing air to be pulled more deeply into your lungs. In addition, the nose has various mechanisms to help warm and filter the air, preventing impurities and excessively cold air from entering the body.

• Whenever possible, it's best to close your eyes. This allows you to switch off and disconnect from the external physical world and draw your attention deep within, reconnecting you with your divine inner source of strength, courage, and creative energy. If you notice your mind starting to wander, bring your attention back to your breath.

• Initially, it's a good idea to reserve a few minutes of each day to practice breathing as a formal discipline. In the morning when you wake up and before you go to sleep are usually good times. After you feel comfortable with it, you can practice breathing at any time of day—while waiting for a bus, taking a break at work, walking around your neighborhood, or whenever. Breathing is particularly useful in frustrating or stressful situations, as it is beneficial for replenishing depleted energy.

- By integrating the breathing exercise above into your life, you'll learn how to absorb far more oxygen and life-force energy. It will help develop your lungs and chest and improve your overall health. With regular practice, your brain will automatically take over, and implement this improved method of breathing into your daily routine. It will become habit, performed naturally throughout the day and while you sleep. Be patient and persistent in your attempts to correct your breathing. The aim is to make this new breathing process a normal and natural part of your life.

Surround and shower yourself
with divine light and energy!

Chapter 18

Energy Emanations

The most profound way we can experience the expansiveness of energy within our body is to attain the ultimate state of oneness.

Everything in the universe consists predominantly of energy. The sharing of this subtle energy is the basis for life and human interaction, and interconnects the ultimate state of oneness. We all live in this energy field; there is no escape. We're constantly transferring and absorbing energy with everyone and everything, unless we decide differently. This energy can have positive, negative—and on occasion—neutral vibrations. Energy can affect us on many levels—spiritually, physically, emotionally, and mentally, so it's important that we understand how energy works and become more aware of our personal energy field. Doing so will give us a deeper understanding of ourselves and how our energy interacts and relates with others. This allows us to make conscious choices about how we use and manage our energy.

As human beings, our essence or core—which is made up of energy—extends out and surrounds the physical body, creating an energy field often referred to as our *aura* or *personal space*. Personal space is an area or region that we respectfully claim as our own. It is a boundary that keeps us safe from intimate or social intrusion. This space may vary in proximity according to who wishes to enter it. We all possess a unique energy field with an intelligence of its own, which acts to serve us should someone step into our personal space. We're able to sense what feels comfortable and safe, and what requires protection. Basically, our energy field is an extension of the subtle energies within our body; and is constantly changing shape and color to reflect our thoughts, feelings, and moods. It is multilayered and has a physical, emotional, mental, and spiritual aspect. Our energy is constantly interacting with the physical world and the energy fields of others.

Everything and everyone we come into contact with holds its own unique energy that vibrates at a particular frequency. Due to the strong electromagnetic properties of energy, we're constantly transferring energy back and forth in the form of energy vibrations with everything and everyone. We can emit energy as well as absorb it from others, and our individual energy system is constantly infringed upon in such subtle ways that it can alter our own personal vibration. Each time we connect with someone or something—either physically, mentally, emotionally, or spiritually—we also link with that energy, allowing a potential exchange or transfer to take place. Similarly, each time someone or something connects with us, that energy also links with ours. Once again we allow a potential exchange or transfer of energy to take place. The more people and objects we connect or associate with, the greater the potential arises for these energy exchanges to occur. This is why people often feel drained and exhausted after dealing with large groups of people.

But it's not only people who can affect our energy. Every image we see, word we speak or hear, scent we smell, thing we taste or touch, thought we have, and emotion we experience has the potential to influence and alter our personal energy vibration. Some of this energy can be positive and have a nurturing effect; other energy can be negative and have a harmful or undesired effect. It is, therefore, very important that we become more aware of our own energy field and understand how it interacts with other people and things. This awareness will help us learn how to prevent certain people and situations from having an ill effect on us.

Our energy is constantly reacting and changing according to what is going on within and around us. This invisible exchange of energy can often subconsciously or consciously affect us and disturb our personal vibration, impacting the way we feel, think, and conduct ourselves. Energy isn't usually visible, but this exchange of energy can often instinctively be sensed or subtly experienced by ourselves and others.

We all have the ability to sense and experience energy within our body and around us. Sometimes it may feel good and inspiring, and other times it may feel unpleasant and draining. The reason is that some people, places, and objects are positive and complement our energy, while others are negative and drain or deplete us. What people or objects radiate or exude usually depends on their nature and character. If, for example, we're greedy, we will radiate greed. If we're generous, we'll radiate generosity. If we're loving, we radiate love; hence, we can learn a lot about ourselves and others by learning to read and sense our energy field.

We're constantly interacting and transferring energy through our connection with others. When we associate with positive people, we create energy based in love and compassion. Through negative connections and interactions, our energy very often feels drained, and so a negative effect is created.

When we connect with positive people, places, or things, we generally feel energized and inspired. By and large, we sense an expansiveness of energy within our body, creating an elevated feeling of love, joy, and happiness. In contrast, when we connect or link with negative people, places, or things, we usually feel drained, uneasy, and possibly even threatened or frightened. In these situations, we usually tend to contract our energy. This can often create unnecessary tension and stiffness within the body. This tension can often lead to headaches, tight shoulders, sweaty palms, or sudden feelings of agitation.

So, we need to pay attention to the signals our body sends, particularly in the presence of negative energy. This effect is not just simply our imagination; it is a genuine registry of energy transference between two or more things, and is usually spirit's way of informing us that something is wrong. Intuitively, we recognize this and are generally drawn to associate with people, places, or things that vibrate on a similar frequency.

Energy will naturally attract and bond to that which is similar to its own frequency, and will react and adjust to that which is not of the same frequency. When the frequency of our energy is close to that of others, we generally experience a familiar and comfortable feeling. With such people, we often feel at ease right away and tend to expand our energy field. On the other hand, when the frequency of our energy is different from that of others, we may feel uncomfortable and experience an unfamiliar feeling.

The subtle impressions that we emit and receive generally reflect the way our personal energy field interacts and harmonizes with that of others. If we experience an uncomfortable or unpleasant feeling, it may not necessarily mean that the person or thing is bad, but simply that our energy is different and not in resonance with that person or thing at that moment in time. For example, we may pick up a book and don't feel drawn to read it. It may not mean that the book isn't interesting or not meant for us; it may simply be the wrong book for us at that particular time. Several months later, we may pick up the same book and find ourselves happily engaged in reading it because it's exactly what we need at that time. In life, we will attract to us most strongly those vibrations that are in tune with our own personal frequency. We will also attract experiences and people that complement or mirror our state of being, as energy usually attracts similar energy.

Our world is a swirling mass of energy. We're constantly exchanging energy with everything and anything around us through an act of energy transference. We cannot always escape the vibrations given off by all people and things we come into contact with; however, we can learn to protect ourselves from the undesirable effects. We all have freedom of choice and the power to control how we utilize our energy—as well as what we allow to enter our mind, body, and soul.

I am surrounded by love and light
I am always safe and protected!

Chapter 19

Spiritual Protection

Just as darkness disappears when we switch on a light,
negativity also disappears in the presence of light.

As mentioned in the previous chapter, everything in our world has an energetic factor, and we're constantly interacting and transferring energy with others. When we're unaware of this energy transference and do little to protect our energy field, we leave ourselves open, which unconsciously exposes our aura to a state of vulnerability. This allows us to absorb positive as well as negative energy.

It's important that we learn to protect ourselves from this type of energy. This doesn't mean that we need to live in a protective bubble, isolated from the rest of the world, trying to avoid everything and everyone, as this will only restrict the flow of energy and the opportunities available to us. It simply means becoming more consciously aware, and learning to recognize the difference between positive and negative energy. This knowledge enables us to protect ourselves from negative energy, and prevent it from invading our personal energy field.

When we link or connect with someone or something, we also begin to pick up on that person or thing's energy. If we're aware, well-balanced, and centered individuals, we'll usually be able to identify and differentiate between that energy and our own and make a conscious choice whether or not to allow it to interact with ours. On the other hand, if we're unaware of this energy exchange, we can often mistake these subtle vibrations and shifts in energy as our own, allowing negative energy to invade our personal energy field—affecting what we think, feel, and do.

In order to take greater control of our life, we need to become more consciously aware of the impact of energy; and how thoughts, people, and things can disturb our personal vibration. This is comparable to leaving the front door to our home open. We don't tend to do so because if we do, anyone and anything could enter. It would be lovely to have this type of openness, but unfortunately in the world we live, it is not advisable. Such openness could attract undesirable people and things, so we have a responsibility to exercise discernment. We close our front door and control who's allowed to enter—usually by invitation or by virtue of familiarity. Similarly, we need to learn to protect our energy field, preventing uninvited energies and entities from invading and interfering with our personal vibration.

If we make a habit of being well balanced, centered, and focused in every moment, we're more likely to recognize when we're thrown off balance by influences outside of ourselves. Our energy will suddenly start to feel different. We can then take charge of and protect our energy field, preventing any potential or harmful energy from coming in.

Similarly, if there's a knock at the front door and we know the person standing there and feel comfortable, we happily welcome this individual into our home. On the other hand, if we don't know this person and feel uncomfortable, we usually exercise caution or discernment and do not allow free access without careful examination or validation.

In general, the easiest way to protect ourselves from negative people, places, situations, and harmful energy is by using the power of our mind and spirit to control the way our mind and soul interacts with others; and make conscious choices about what we let in and out of our life. The most successful, visionary, and innovative individuals maintain control of their mind and thoughts constantly.

If we like something or someone and feel comfortable, we can send a subconscious or conscious message to the mind to stay open and continue to receive and enjoy such energies. When we dislike something or someone and feel uncomfortable, we can send a message to the mind to close and detach ourselves from the situation.

Peace of mind is usually directly connected to the energy we allow ourselves to emit and receive. By learning to recognize what energizes us and what drains us, we can learn to ward off negative and draining influences. With practice, patience, and discipline, this will become a natural and automatic response. Our energy centers will naturally begin to open and close depending on what is happening within and around us.

In order to protect ourselves, it's vital that we stay mentally alert and learn to monitor and control our thoughts in every moment. If we do so, there's very little anyone or anything can do to affect us. We're poised to protect ourselves purely through the power of our mind and our intention.

Our energy is not physical, although the same concept applies as opening and closing the front door to our home. When we feel comfortable and safe, we allow our energy to open and expand. Conversely, when we feel uncomfortable and threatened in some way, we contract and close our energy field. There's no specific way to do this; it simply involves our awareness, and our intention to protect ourselves.

Intention is a very creative and powerful force. If our

intention is to protect ourselves from negative energy, then we're *automatically* protected. If, on the other hand, we believe we can be harmed or affected by negative energy, we tend to unconsciously lower our energy vibration, creating holes in our energy field through which negative energy can pass, affecting our personal vibration. Love and light is the opposite of fear and darkness. Fear tends to wear down our guard, making us more susceptible to negativity.

The most effective form of protection is a strong energy field that radiates love, light, and vitality. It is, therefore, a good idea to engage in a regular practice that helps clear, strengthen, and protect our energy field. Positive affirmations are a powerful way to strengthen it and reinforce our intention for protection. We can think or state positive affirmations such as "I am always surrounded with white light, love, and protection"; or "I am protected every day, in every way." The key is to experiment with affirmations that feel comfortable and right for you.

Creative visualization is another useful technique that can help us strengthen and protect our energy field. We can do this by simply visualizing an egg-shaped sphere of white light or some other form of protection that completely surrounds us from head to toe, creating a solid barrier that negativity cannot pass through. We can then imagine any negative energy that is directed toward us bouncing off the shield and reflecting back to the source of negativity with love, light, and healing power. The shield can be used when we find ourselves in compromising situations, and is an effective way to reinforce and strengthen our intention for protection. This method can also be used to protect loved ones and objects that are of value to us, and helps us build a strong shield that is with us for all time.

We can also prepare ourselves for difficult or compromising situations by creating a type of prompt that automatically helps us remain strong, centered, and focused. In doing so, we're not easily thrown off balance by other people's opinions, beliefs, actions, and expectations. This may simply be a word or mantra we repeat to ourselves, a simple action, a memory, or some other type of trigger that allows us to remain focused and true to ourselves at all times, regardless of the situation we may find ourselves in. It may even just involve switching off or diverting our attention away from whatever it is that may be causing the upset or disturbance. If we cannot see, feel, taste, smell, or hear it, it's less likely to impact us.

It's important to find a type of protection that works for you as an individual—something that can be summoned in an instant whenever you feel threatened or find yourself in a compromising situation. It's also a good idea to adopt a regular energy-cleansing practice to clear out any negative energy that may have accumulated during the day, or cleanse cobwebs that may have formed over time.

Clearing our energy field simply involves cleansing the spiritual, mental, and emotional layers of our aura from negative energies that are present or have accumulated. In the same way that we take a shower to cleanse our physical body, we can do the same thing for our aura with energetic cleansing. It helps remove negative energies and impurities, preventing them from building up and having an ill effect on us. It also restores the natural, healthy flow of energy within and around our body, strengthening our energy field.

There are various clearing and cleansing techniques and practices that we can employ. A simple and effective one we can do while we're in the shower is to imagine the water cleansing and clearing our energy as well as our physical body. It's worth remembering that our intention is a very creative force, and by simply *intending* to cleanse our aura, we will, in fact, help to clear, purify, and strengthen it. As we become more confident and proficient, we can begin to use our intuition to help guide us to any areas of our body or energy field that may need particular attention—directing our focus to that specific area with the intention of eliminating negative energy.

In our everyday lives, we're constantly exposed to positive

as well as negative forms of energy. It almost seems like it's a constant struggle to rise above these lower vibrations and prevent them from affecting our inner peace and calm. The best form of protection is to stay mentally focused on our heart's true desires and divine life purpose, and to live in the light of higher truth.

When we're doing what we're destined to do, the universe will naturally support and protect us. When we consciously choose to live and fulfill our divine life purpose, there's very little that anyone else can do to stop us. Truth is a powerful weapon and can help us overcome even the most difficult situations. When we choose to live in the light of higher truth, we can more easily recognize and dispel negative energy, raising our personal vibration to higher levels of consciousness. Darkness cannot penetrate light. Our spirit has the power to dispel and transmute negative energy into light. Just as darkness disappears when we switch the light on in a dark room, negativity also disappears in the presence of light.

The more we hold on to the light deep within the core of our being, the more light we allow to enter into our life. This naturally provides us with all the necessary strength and courage to live our inner truth, and also keeps us from being easily affected or thrown off balance by the negativity that exists in our world today.

Deep within resides a precious jewel
Waiting to be revealed

Deep within resides a bright light
Waiting to shine in all its brilliance

Deep within resides a limitless well
Where unconditional love and peace prevail

Deep within resides a divine wisdom and superior intelligence
Where inner peace and tranquility dwell

Deep within resides a deep silence
Where truth and honesty prevail

Deep within resides a deep stillness
Where time and space cease to exist

Deep within resides an indescribable beauty
Full of marvel and wonder

Deep within resides an infinite source of creative power
Where anything is possible

Deep within resides a deeper yearning
Waiting to be free!

Chapter 20

Self-Realization

The higher the climb, the better the view when we reach the summit!

Life is a continuous journey filled with adventure, opportunities and, most important, self-realization. The term *self-realization* is a translation of *Atman Jnana*, which is Sanskrit for "knowledge of true self." *Atman* refers to the soul, and *Jnana* refers to knowledge gained from personal experience, as opposed to mere intellectual knowledge or that which we may acquire from reading a book. We choose to come back to the Earth plane or physical level of existence because we still have certain lessons to learn, enabling us to evolve spiritually, and positively contribute to the evolution of our planet.

When we're born, we're stripped of any conscious awareness of our divinity and our infinite source of creative power. It is through our experiences that we're given the grand opportunity to reveal our deepest desires and rediscover the all-encompassing divine consciousness within our being. Self-realization is the pathway to enlightenment, eternal freedom, and liberation.

There's no greater misfortune than a lack of awareness of our divine inner being and infinite source of creative power. In fact, most of our problems, including suffering, pain, worry, anxiety, and limitations, can usually be attributed to, or emerge from, our lack of knowledge concerning our true nature and ultimate state of being—that is, the all-inspiring and luminous part of us that exists independently from our physical, mental, emotional, and personal state of affairs. Our true nature is composed of pure consciousness and eternal bliss. We all possess this knowledge deep within the core of our being, which is why we usually cannot settle for any type of limitation to our existence and are, therefore, constantly seeking to improve our lives. We desperately yearn to experience the all-embracing love, joy, and fulfillment of our spirit.

The problem is, however, that too often we allow external factors and our empirical existence to dictate and influence our motives in life, which then tend to overshadow our spirit and true desires. Unfortunately, most of the prevailing systems in our modern world tend to disregard the energetic or spiritual part of our being, and as a result, we're forced to look outside ourselves for happiness and fulfillment.

When we neglect the energetic part of our being, we can become trapped and deluded within the illusion of our physical existence. Then, we too often allow ourselves to get entangled in the materialistic nature of our world, and become emotionally involved in our daily situations, giving them strength and power. The more we focus on our physical existence, striving for material advancement and pleasure, the more we become caught up in the temporary illusions and allure of the superficial world. This makes it difficult for us to free ourselves from material entrapments, a state that is not conducive to our divine life purpose and which defeats the intent of our earthly existence. Material pleasure is merely a momentary form of mental stimulation and excitement of the physical senses. Ideally, we should seek to engage in life for the joy inherent in the transcendental senses—and not just the physical ones.

The material world and physical body are temporary forms of existence, and if we strictly engage in life to satisfy this type of pleasure, we're bound by temporary things. Also, when we depend strictly on our external reality to provide happiness and fulfillment, we're again governed by temporary concerns. We may experience moments of happiness and ecstasy, but these are usually short-lived because they depend on factors outside of ourselves and often leave us feeling worse when they fade away or disappear. We may already know what we need to do in order to improve our life, but simply lack the courage, inner strength, and motivation to actually put it into practice.

On the other hand, if we engage in life to rediscover and live our inner truth, then we're involved in something permanent. It's important to remember that we won't find eternal bliss and fulfillment in situations and circumstances outside ourselves. True beauty and joy come from within, by honoring our genuine desires and living our truth—not our external possessions and situations. More important, happiness stems from realizing the truth of our highest and purest state of being.

Most of us identify the self with our body and mind. The higher or true self, however, is pure awareness and consciousness, devoid of thoughts and individual identification (ego) of any kind. This higher self, therefore, cannot be accessed through the mind. It exists independent of our emotional, physical, and mental self and must be realized through experience. It is only through releasing our earthbound attachments that we can come to realize the truth of our ultimate state of existence without allowing our ego, emotions, fears, expectations, and desires get in the way and cloud our experience.

The mind can be observed or witnessed by our higher self, although it exists beyond the reasoning or logic of the mind.

The mind can be purified and perfected. The higher self, however, is not subject to such control. It is already perfect and whole. It is absolute consciousness and pure bliss, free of any thoughts whatsoever. It is an expansive and all-encompassing state of being that exists beyond form, time, and space. Therefore, it is not easily translated into words; it must be realized through experience.

Self-realization is the process that enables us to pierce through the illusion of our physical existence and gain awareness of the truth of our radiant inner self. It involves the peeling back or shedding of the many layers of our physical existence in order to reveal the ultimate truth of our unaltered state of being, which has been seriously impinged upon by our physical reality. When we become fully aware of our higher self, we unleash the infinite possibilities and potential of our spirit, which is already perfect and complete. It is eternal, divine, and all-knowing. When we truly comprehend this simple truth, we no longer need to hide in the shadows of our ego; we become free to bathe in the magical, all-revealing, and self-illuminating light of our spirit.

Our actual spiritual journey begins with the realization of our higher self. Once the connection has been established, it needs to be cultivated through our conscious awareness and mindfulness. Self-realization is an eternal journey of self-inquiry and inner exploration, which offers us an infinite source of wisdom and knowledge. If we get to the point where we think we know it all, we become imprisoned in the ego's realm of illusion.

Every moment in life provides us with an opportunity to transcend our physical level of existence and use our inner power to create our desired reality. In life, it is not our situations and circumstances that are important, but how we handle them and what they reveal and teach us about ourselves. Our situations act like great teachers, encouraging us to probe deeper within ourselves, unearthing the clarity and understanding we seek and desire. We will all attract particular people, events, and situations in order to help us reconnect with the truth of our divine inner being, allowing us to explore our heart, mind, and soul. What we attract will very often depend on the stage of our spiritual evolvement— lessons we still need to learn in order to fulfill our divine purpose and live a spiritually awakened and empowered life. Thus, it is not the *situations* that are important, but the *realizations* that are very often disguised in them.

There are no good or bad occurrences—but only our ideas and acquired beliefs about what we *consider* to be good or bad. Quite often, the situations that we consider to be the most difficult actually teach us the most. They guide us toward change, and ultimately, self-realization. Usually, it's not until we've exhausted all external avenues and have hit rock bottom that we're forced to look deep within ourselves. It is here that we'll find all the unconditional love, clarity, peace, and fulfillment that we've yearned for.

What we enter this world with, we leave it with—nothing more, nothing less. Everything we need and seek is already a part of us. It is only when we come to this realization that we ultimately find true peace, contentment, and satisfaction. When we comprehend this simple truth, we appreciate that all else is merely superficial. With this understanding, our perspective dramatically begins to change, and we can start to view our situations and circumstances differently. Therefore, there's no need to rush, stress, or allow ourselves to be caught up in constantly trying to achieve more. Sometimes less is more, and this understanding affords us the space and time to freely enjoy each moment.

Self-realization is a lifelong process that constantly tests us and provides choices and opportunities for growth and development. Due to the nature of our earthly existence, obstacles are inevitable. When faced with adversity on this truly grand voyage, we should not be discouraged. Life can't always be easy; if this were the case, it would defeat the purpose of our earthly existence. We need to appreciate that there will be difficult times and challenges that guide us toward self-realization. We need to learn to welcome these times and regard them as opportunities for growth and spiritual evolvement. Every difficulty or struggle is an opportunity for us to grow stronger in will and realize the truth of our ultimate state of existence.

In times of darkness, difficulty, and despair, we need to find the stillness deep within our being as a source of comfort, guidance, strength, and support. The longer we reside within this powerful center, the more peace and clarity we will unearth, allowing us to deal with difficult situations with greater ease, joy, and satisfaction. Although the spiritual path isn't always easy, it is always rewarding and fulfilling.

The path to self-realization requires immense focus, effort, commitment, patience, honesty, trust, discipline, inner strength, and dedication in order to reach a higher state of consciousness and the realization of oneself. However, once attained, the rewards are limitless, enabling us to experience a state of peace and tranquility not easily encapsulated into words alone.

In order to achieve our loftiest desires, we must rise above the material allure and entrapment of the modern world. The secret lies in always being conscious of our divinity and maintaining a spiritual connection in every moment. We all have the innate potential to transform ourselves for the better and so, attain a profound sense of joy and contentment. We simply need to believe in ourselves and remember that love needs to be the basis for all we do. The most spiritually minded and empowered people are often the most peaceful and blissful. They are profoundly aware of their divine inner consciousness, and are constantly seeking to achieve and maintain a high level of self-realization.

Follow your inner bliss
And attain your ultimate reality!

Chapter 21

Enlightenment

Trust, Surrender, and Believe.

Enlightenment is a state of higher consciousness where time, space, and other constrictive realities that are part of our physical existence fail to exist. In this state, this level of illumination allows us to experience life from beyond its earthly limitations. Enlightenment involves the transcendence of the mind and the physical world, enabling us to experience our true fundamental nature and dwell in the realms of pure consciousness, ultimate knowledge, and ineffable beauty. It is a profound experience that is naturally accompanied by a sense of inner peace and tranquility, free from the suffering and torment that is often common to our physical existence. It is a place where circumstances, habits, thoughts, and other earthly states do not exist; nor do they disturb, impact, or unsettle our inner peace and harmony.

This enlightened state of being is not something that exists outside ourselves, and so, is not something that needs to be obtained or acquired; it is already intrinsic to our natural state of being.

Enlightenment refers to a higher state of consciousness, and in its literal sense, translates to "one who has accomplished his or her ultimate reality." When we attain a state of enlightenment, we release ourselves from earthly limitations. It is a state of being beyond form, where anything and everything is possible. Enlightenment is total freedom and liberation of the spirit. In order to attain this highly evolved state, we must rid ourselves of any selfish desires that are associated with the physical world. Enlightenment is a state whereby personality and character do not have a place. The ego disappears, along with all identification with the mind and body.

Enlightenment is experienced in this life as a dissolution of the sense of self as an egoistic personality. It encompasses freedom from erroneous concepts, beliefs, opinions, and ideas, which too often lower our vibration solely to the physical level of existence. Enlightenment is a state of utter peace of mind—free of cravings, anger, anxieties, worries, and other afflictive states. This peace, which, in essence, is the fundamental nature of the mind, is revealed when the root causes of these afflictive states are dissolved. It is a state where absolutely nothing or no one can disturb our inner peace, even in the midst of our greatest challenges. Enlightenment is a state of being where all desires cease, and one attains total freedom and liberation of the soul. It is a paradox in the sense that overcoming desires also involves rising above the desire for enlightenment itself!

Enlightenment is a state of consciousness that exists in a dimension transcending time and space. Therefore, it's impossible to define or even ponder. It involves a sense of utter and complete peace and stillness of mind, devoid of any thoughts whatsoever. In the state of enlightenment, the mind that loves to define and label everything is simply not a part of the picture, and so, is unable to describe or grasp it properly. As long as we try to understand or perceive enlightenment, we merely separate ourselves further and can never really truly experience it. Enlightenment will occur when attachment has fallen away. It requires us to simply let go and live.

In order to attain enlightenment, we must go beyond the mind and the physical world. It requires us to surrender and release any personal or individual identification associated with our physical reality. This isn't always easy, as the rational mind likes to hold on to this experience. It is only when we've conquered the mind that we can truly revel in this part of our being that is already perfect, all-knowing, eternal, and beyond physical form.

Seeking spiritual enlightenment is a lifelong commitment, but everyone with the desire can experience it. However, as human beings occupying a physical body, it isn't always possible to maintain such a state of being 24 hours a day, every day. The reason is that this state of unity means that we lose all individuality and personal identity, with no need for anything physical whatsoever—we are 100 percent spirit. EnLIGHTenment simply means that we become light over matter. But most of us are so engrossed in our daily existence that the idea of detaching ourselves and giving ourselves completely to such desires seems unrealistic. More important, as long as we choose to live in the physical world, we need our mind and body to interact emotionally, physically, and mentally with this plane of existence.

As human beings living a physical existence, we consist of a mind, body, and spirit. Although it's important to hold on to the experience of enlightenment, we also need to integrate the mind and body in order to live a happy and fulfilling life. Maintaining a balance of mind, body, and spirit is absolutely essential to living a spiritually awakened and empowered life. The three are interconnected; a weakness or imbalance in one area can affect the others.

The body acts as a wonderful transport vehicle that enables us to carry out our divine life purpose. The mind is like the steering wheel of a car or a highly sophisticated navigational system that we control and program. The spirit is our ultimate driving force, similar to the fuel that powers a car.

Although enlightenment is not the most practical state of being to maintain 24 hours a day, it is still the highest and most worthy objective that we should strive to attain in this physical life. It means consciously and fully awakening to the light that is deep within the core of our being. A truly enlightened person knows that true power comes from a connection with our universal source, which connects all life on our planet and beyond, creating an ultimate state of oneness.

We all have the power to let go of the countless thoughts running through our mind. The key is to learn to trust, surrender, and believe, exploring what it's like to truly let go and just simply *be*. It is our mind and ego that hold on to suffering and pain. Enlightenment is knowing that this awesome universal intelligence and power is always present, in every moment, guiding us every step of the way. Enlightened souls naturally become at one with the universe and always live in the light of higher truth. They also have a strong desire to help others rediscover this truth within themselves, for when we realize this truth within ourselves, we can help others find it as well. This domino effect is the key to establishing peace, balance, and harmony in our world today.

May Darkness be overcome by Light
Sorrow by Joy
Negativity by Positivity
Ignorance by Knowledge
Innocence by Wisdom
Weakness by Strength
Fear by Courage
Hurt by Forgiveness
Anger by Understanding
Resentment by Compassion
Chaos by Peace
Greed by Generosity
Cruelty by Kindness
Disease by Ease
Illness by Health
Lack by Abundance
Confusion by Clarity
Doubt by Faith
Despair by Hope
Worry by Trust

Chapter 22

True Empowerment

Rediscover all the love, peace, and happiness inherent in the power of the spirit.

Spiritual empowerment is a highly focused, resourceful, and heightened state of being. We become spiritually empowered when we realize the truth of our divine inner being and begin to live an awakened life. Our spirit or energy has the power and knowledge to miraculously transform all our trials and tribulations. The more we realize and nurture our unity with spirit, the more empowered we become, allowing us to operate in the world from a center of stability, deeply anchored in this part of our being.

Self-realization and spiritual empowerment hold the keys to eternal freedom and liberation, free of our own self-imposed limitations and the inconsiderate impositions of others. When we connect with the spiritual part of our being, we experience a profound sense of inner peace and purpose. This is an empowering experience, as it's the beginning of realizing the incredible power and potential we already possess to miraculously change our world and create our desired reality. Self-realization and spiritual empowerment are the bases for genuine love, selfless service, and an enlightened life.

In our physical form of existence, it's virtually impossible to be without desire. It is simply the nature and drive of the human being. We're constantly striving to improve our lives, so a person without desire is usually viewed as lifeless and passive, lacking in motivation and direction. The key, therefore, to living a spiritually awakened life is to transfer our desires from serving the illusion of our physical existence to serving the truth of our ultimate reality. In everyone's life there are two dualities: one to serve the illusion, and the other to serve the reality.

The substance of our world is that of duality. For example, summer and sunshine can exist in one moment, and then, winter can descend with cold and rain. Similarly, in one moment we can experience ecstasy and happiness; and in the next, misery and misfortune. Unless we experience and understand one side of the equation, we won't appreciate and understand its opposite. In essence, it's not possible to understand *progression* unless we've experienced *regression*.

However, spiritually empowered individuals aren't subject to such dualities, as they see everything as the same, and all people as equal. The state of higher consciousness is merely freedom from illusion, affording the ability to live our true, idyllic, eternal nature. Spiritually empowered individuals are, therefore, unphased by the allure of the world, and are calm and at peace with themselves and the natural rhythms and laws of the universe. They maintain a strong spiritual connection in every moment, and consciously choose to see the world through the eyes of the spirit, keeping their mind focused on serving the truth of reality. The material world has no appeal or attraction, as all is equal.

When we choose to view the world through the eyes of our spirit, our inspiration and motivation for life instinctively begin to change. We naturally reconnect with the spiritual part of our being, experiencing a greater perspective on life and, as a result, a profound sense of inner peace and tranquility. This shift in consciousness allows us to become more acutely aware of our total self, which positively affects our state of mind and innermost being.

This experience is empowering, as it is only when we know who we really are and what we truly desire in life that we can we begin to use our energy and power to make the best decisions and choices for ourselves. This brings us into closer alignment with our higher self and the infinite creative power of the universe. An inner journey is, therefore, an essential prerequisite to truly living a spiritually empowered life, as it naturally propagates the greatest transformation in our self-confidence and perspective. This equips us with the necessary tools to live our life in a more fulfilling and all-encompassing manner. The difficult part, however, often arises when we try to integrate this heightened state of being into our daily life, without neglecting our worldly responsibilities or succumbing to the materialistic allure and negative influences that are omnipresent.

To maintain this blissful and heightened state of being in a world that constantly demands our attention and challenges our existence, requires immense spiritual strength and willpower. The key, therefore, is to be consciously aware of the power deep within the core of our being and to maintain a spiritual connection in every moment. This requires us to operate from a center of stability deeply anchored in this part of our being—a place greater than the trivial details of life. So, when things go wrong, as they sometimes do, we're able to remain focused and connected to our divine inner source of power, inspiration, and strength.

A strong spiritual connection allows us to rise above everyday challenges and view them from a higher perspective where we can gain insight into their true nature. This equips us with tools such as compassion, forgiveness, patience, tolerance, and strength, which will enable us to address and move through them in a positive way. The longer we abide in this center, the more light we reveal, allowing our divine life purpose to be easily perceived and maintained. This is an empowering experience that provides us with the necessary strength and courage to remain true to ourselves at all times, allowing us to stand firm and strong in our beliefs and to take the necessary steps to realize our dreams and attain our ultimate reality.

We become spiritually empowered when we're truly free to live life as an authentic expression of our higher self. This means being honest with ourselves and having the courage and strength to follow our heart's true desires. We need to believe in ourselves and in the incredible power of the universe to guide us, always working for our highest intentions. It also means freely speaking and expressing our truth, absent of fear; yet at the same time always being considerate, gentle, and sensitive toward others. Deep within our being is our pure consciousness, which is the part of us that knows our true desires and is always guiding us toward greater love, peace, happiness, and fulfillment. If we deceive ourselves or anyone else, we won't have a clear conscience. This can affect our inner peace and create a troubled state of mind, which is the spirit's way of letting us know that something is wrong.

When we compromise or deny our spirit or true desires— usually from fear or lack of trust—we disconnect from our divine inner source of power. As a result, energy will begin to leak, making us more susceptible to the negative influences that exist in our world today. In order to maintain this heightened state of being, we need to become more aware of what causes leakages in our energy, and be vigilant in order to protect ourselves from negative or harmful external influences.

When we remain true to ourselves and open our heart to love through compassion and selfless service, we're automatically protected and nourished by our divine source of creative power, and begin to act as pure channels of radiant and abundant energy. This is the divine energy that connects us with the incredible wisdom deep within ourselves—the infinite source of power and creative energy of the universe, and the divine spark of light within others.

To truly live a spiritually empowered life, we must learn to take greater control of our inner selves and assume responsibility for the management of our energy. We must become more consciously aware of the thoughts and beliefs that we allow to dwell in our mind. We need to learn to use our inborn creative power to collectively improve the quality of life on our planet. This prevents us from giving in to the authority of misleading influences and the allure of our physical world, which too often binds our creative energy in chains, preventing us from truly realizing our dreams.

True spiritual empowerment comes from being able to control our mind, thoughts, and physical senses. If we don't learn to monitor and control what we think, we give away our power and allow others to easily influence how we think and what we do. Spiritually empowered individuals aren't dependent on the dictates of the mind; rather, the mind comes under *their* control. True empowerment involves relying on our inner self and allowing the inner promptings of our heart and higher consciousness to determine our motives in life, as opposed to the ordinary consciousness of the intellect. As we become more spiritually aware, we can empower ourselves to make choices in life that nurture and serve our higher self.

True empowerment is not only about empowering ourselves, but also about reaching out to others with compassion, sincerity, and humility. When we realize this truth within ourselves, we also begin to recognize it in others, and are now in a stronger position to help them become aware of their own inner source of power. But in our attempts to aid others, it is essential that we do not become overly involved or meddle in their lives. Over-attachment can be detrimental to our well-being and can also drain our personal resources and energy. At the same time, it's important to realize that when we commit to living a spiritually awakened life, acting as selfless channels, we're naturally rewarded with more energy, and all that we need in order to fulfill our divine life purpose.

Our spirit is nonjudgmental and strives to undo the wrongs in the world and aid in the recovery of others. Our spirit, due to its innate nature, performs kind, selfless deeds without expectation. Our spirit is aware of its divine interconnectedness to all living things and seeks to reunite with its counterparts to live in perfect bliss and harmony.

We become empowered when we understand that human beings are all different and deserve respect, regardless of their status or position in life. Everybody is intrinsically good and has the potential to shine. A spiritually aware person can see beyond character and identify with the spark of goodness deep within every soul, and emanate sincere compassion for everybody and everything. We begin to develop tremendous love and self-respect for both ourselves and others, which will be reflected in everything we do and say. Our relationships become more authentic, satisfying, and peaceful, leading to more harmonious relations with one and all— including ourselves.

The key to true empowerment is to learn to let go of everything, and experience what it is like to simply *be*. Only when we trust, surrender, and believe in the incredible power of our spirit, which is all-knowing, all-powerful, and all-creative, can we start to see things happen in miraculous and mysterious ways. This experience is empowering, as it enables us to readily relinquish our human need to try to control everything, allowing our spirit to make the right things occur in the right order and time.

Spiritually empowered people are always humble and modest. They never need to display anger or aggression to acquire anything, as they trust and believe in the universe to always provide what they need in life in the right time and place. As a result, they never need to lie, hurt, steal, or manipulate anyone or anything for their own selfish gain. These qualities exist only to disconnect us from our divine source of inner peace and power. Such behavior merely demonstrates a lack of spiritual awareness, knowledge, and self-respect. Spiritually empowered beings appreciate that they're already whole and complete, wherever they may be and whatever they do.

When we trust, surrender, and believe in the incredible wisdom and power of our spirit, we'll be guided to always create for our highest good. Life will naturally begin to unfold with greater ease, prosperity, and fulfillment. Our spirit naturally strives for a higher existence separate from darkness, despair, and destruction. Spiritually empowered individuals always feel safe and secure, and rest in the knowledge of spirit. They're never shaken, even in the midst of the greatest difficulties.

Unfortunately, the world we live in has much strife and is in need of redemption, which refers to forgiveness, recovery, and deliverance from our previous mistakes. Humanity appears to have lost its direction in terms of kindness, compassion, empathy, and regard for civilization as a whole. We're currently experiencing the result of centuries of human ignorance, greed, and the accumulation of all our negative thoughts and actions. Most people have disconnected from their divine source of power, and as a result, have become entangled in the allure of the modern world.

It seems that we're often blind to the misfortune and selfishness that exists within our world. If we're going to do anything to change our current situation, we need to reawaken ourselves to our true nature. We inherently have the potential to work together and create a higher level of existence. True spiritual empowerment isn't just an individual pursuit or an isolated experience. When one person experiences enlightenment and learns to live a truly spiritually empowered life, this individual not only begins to change him- or herself for the better, but begins to radiate genuine sincerity and compassion for life. This is highly infectious and inspiring to everyone whom these people meet or come in contact with.

One of the greatest gifts given to humanity is the freedom of choice, and we all have the power to effect positive change. In much the same way, we can do nothing and continue to maintain the status quo, which creates a domino effect that perpetuates the same old problems, situations, and dilemmas. Alternatively, we can take back control, reclaim our power, and become a dynamic force in the creation of our reality. In fact, the new world depends on the willingness of each and every one of us to claim greater responsibility for our life.

We already possess the power to transform the world in which we live through love, positive thinking, and action. We have the means and capacity to awaken to the truth of our innate potential and rise above the negativity that exists today. We *come* from light; therefore, it only makes sense that we should *live* in light. We need to trust, surrender, and believe in our spiritual self and the higher powers of the universe. Self-realization and spiritual empowerment hold the key to eternal freedom and liberation. A spiritually empowered person lives an all-embracing life filled with unconditional love, selfless service, and compassion. Such people are always living in the light of higher truth.

The responsibility is ours! Our future and that of our planet depend on it. The time has come for change. It is time to take back our personal power and become proactive forces in the creation of our reality.

Believe in the power and beauty of your dreams, and go forward to live the life you truly desire and deserve!

*** ***

Afterword

Our divine life purpose
Is to nurture our true desires

Our ultimate destination
Is where true riches are stored

Maybe you're a believer
Maybe you're a deceiver

Afraid of the unknown
Afraid to let go

Why do people complicate things?
Why do people try so hard to be?

Follow your dreams
To where true riches are stored

No one wants to be the one who stands alone
A simple shift in mass consciousness

Awaken to the knocking
Cast all fears and doubts aside
Unlock the door
And truly be free!

Gina Zurzolo was born in Melbourne, Australia, and currently lives in the U.K. She is a qualified teacher, author, intuitive healer, and Reiki Master Teacher/Practitioner. Gina has always been interested and committed to the art of healing and the well-being of others. She currently manages her own well-being and healing practice in London, which provides her with a practical means to positively contribute to the healing, teaching, and empowerment of others.

www.wellbeingandhealing.com

13008094R00114

Printed in Great Britain
by Amazon.co.uk, Ltd.,
Marston Gate.